Sunderland College
Bede/Headways Learning Centre

CURIOUS CUSTOMS AND FESTIVALS

*A guide to local customs and festivals
throughout England and Wales*

Martin Green

COUNTRYSIDE BOOKS
NEWBURY, BERKSHIRE

First published 1993
by Impact Books, London
Revised and Updated Edition
published by Countryside Books 2001

COUNTRYSIDE BOOKS
3 Catherine Road
Newbury, Berkshire

To view our complete range of books
please visit us at
www.countrysidebooks.co.uk

ISBN 1 85306 721 0

Photographs, courtesy of Doc Rowe

Produced through MRM Associates Ltd., Reading
Printed by J. W. Arrowsmith, Ltd., Bristol

Contents

Introduction

This guide will tell the reader where and when he or she can see most of the varied traditional customs and festivals in England and Wales. Where known, the historical facts are given, with many of the surmises made about their origins that have arisen over the years. I have read some bizarre interpretations during my research, but have avoided any speculation of my own.

It is tempting to think that most of our colourful and popular customs are a legacy from the 'Merrie England' portrayed in Shakespeare's *Merry Wives of Windsor*, or *Twelfth Night*, and indeed some of them are, such as the Helston Furry Dance or Wassailing the Apple Trees. Most of those recorded in this book, however, spring either from early celebrations marking the passing of the seasons, such as those surrounding the advent of spring or midsummer as at Stonehenge and elsewhere, or from festivities and rites associated with the Christian calendar, as at Christmas and Easter. A number of pre-Christian rites, particularly those associated with the turning of the year, in December and January, have become so closely associated with later Christian rituals that they have been wholly absorbed and are now inseparable from them. Celebrations of Christ's nativity and Yuletide revels are now a continuous festival wherein both traditions are joined.

Dramatic upheavals in our history have had lasting repercussions on our customs and festivals; in particular, the Reformation, which seized the power and patronage of the Church, the abbots and priors of the great monastic orders, and took them firmly under the control of the Crown. Thereafter, there was Cromwell and the Commonwealth, heralding the advent of Puritanism; this was followed shortly afterwards by the Restoration, which retrieved a little part of the earlier harmless merriment, witnesses to which are the number of customs that now take place on Oak Apple Day, the birthday of Charles II.

Most devastating of all, possibly, was the Industrial Revolution, which took the people off the land and drove them into the huge manufacturing cities. Two world wars have also left their marks, the first of which not only wiped out a whole generation, but changed people's very beliefs in a constant and ordered world, where God was in His heaven and all was well below. The second heralded a brave new world of technology and the awesome destructive power of nuclear weapons that has been with us ever since. That we still have such a variety and abundance of popular customs alive today is a tribute to some inherent desire and enthusiasm for celebrating simple pleasures that has defied the onset of manufactured amusement provided by the cinema and television.

Looking over the ground covered in this guide, various threads emerge that are worthy of note. One of the most obvious is the number of street or countryside football games, mostly at Shrovetide but some at other times, which can be witnessed from Ashbourne in Derbyshire down to St Columb Major in Cornwall. On the whole, these appear to be a kind of ritual and mostly bloodless battle between two ends of town or neighbouring villages, echoes of which can be seen in primitive societies as far away as Papua New Guinea. Marking the boundary was a matter of common concern and needed constant vigilance. The beating of the bounds itself is not confined to rural areas and can be witnessed in such cities as Oxford, Lichfield and London.

There is really no satisfactory definition of custom or festival that includes everything covered in this book. Essentially, a custom is an event where people come together to commemorate, celebrate or simply enjoy themselves, at a particular place and a particular time of the year. William Shakespeare, as ever, summed it up when he says in *As You Like It*:

> *Hath not old custom made this life more sweet*
> *Than that of painted pomp?*

And as to why some of these are celebrated, particularly with very little apparent reason for their performance – the Broughton Tin Can Band, for instance – Dylan Thomas, introducing his *Collected Poems*, says:

> 'I read somewhere of a shepherd who, when asked
> why he made from within fairy rings, ritual
> observances to the moon to protect his flocks,
> replied: "I'd be a damn fool if I didn't."'

Note
The map accompanying each entry gives the approximate location of where the event is held.

List of Customs by County

Avon
    Pipe Walk, Bristol

Berkshire
    Hocktide, Hungerford
    Maids' Money, St Mary's Church, Reading
    Marvyn Dole, Ufton Nervet, near Reading

Buckinghamshire
    Firing the Poppers, Fenny Stratford
    Olney Pancake Race, Olney
    Weighing the Mayor, The Guildhall, High Wycombe

Cambridgeshire
    Dicing for Bibles, St Ives
    Straw Bear Day, Whittlesey

Cheshire
    Antrobus Souling Play, Antrobus
    Bawming the Thorn, Appleton, near Warrington

Cornwall
    Helston Furry Dance, Helston
    Hurling, St Columb Major
    Hurling the Silver Ball, St Ives
    John Knill's Charity, St Ives
    Padstow Hobby Horse, Padstow
    Tom Bawcock's Eve, Mousehole

Cumbria
    Appleby Horse Fair, Appleby
    Egremont Crab Fair, Egremont

Derbyshire
    Ashbourne Ball Game, Ashbourne
    Eyam Plague Memorial, Eyam
    Garland Day, Castleton
    Well-Dressing, Tissington

Devon
    Bonfire Night, Ottery St Mary
    Burrator Reservoir Ceremony, near Yelverton

Glove is Up, Honiton
Hunting the Earl of Rone, Combe Martin
Pretty Maid's Charity, Holsworthy
Turning the Devil's Stone, Shebbear, near Holsworthy

Dorset
Abbotsbury Garland Day, Abbotsbury
Purbeck Marblers and Stonecutters Day, Corfe Castle

Durham
Battle of Neville's Cross, Durham Cathedral
Durham Miners' Gala, Durham

Dyfed
Common Walk, Laugharne

Essex
Colchester Oyster Ceremony, Colchester
Dunmow Flitch Trials, Great Dunmow

Glamorgan
Mari Lwyd, Llangynwyd (and elsewhere)

Gloucestershire
Bread and Cheese Throwing, St Briavels
Cheese Rolling, Cooper's Hill, Brockworth
Clipping the Church, Painswick
Cotswold Olympic Games, Chipping Campden
Marshfield Paper Boys, Marshfield

Hampshire
Knights of the Old Green Competition, Southampton
Tichborne Dole, Tichborne
Wayfarers' Dole, St Cross Hospital, Winchester

Hertfordshire
Old Man's Day, Braughing, near Bishop's Stortford

Isle of Man
Tynwald Ceremony, St Johns

Kent
Admiralty Court, Rochester
Biddenden Dole, or Maids' Charity, Biddenden
St Bartholomew's Bun Race, Sandwich

Lancashire
Britannia Coconut Dancers, Bacup

Leicestershire
Hare Pie Scramble and Bottle-Kicking, Hallaton

Lincolnshire
Haxey Hood Game, Haxey

London
Baddeley Cake, Drury Lane Theatre WC2
Blessing the Throats, St Ethelreda, Ely Place EC1
Doggett's Coat and Badge Race, between London and
    Chelsea Bridges
John Stow's Quill Pen, Leadenhall Street EC3
Oranges and Lemons Service, St Clement Danes, Strand WC2
Swearing on the Horns, Old Wrestlers Tavern, Highgate N6
Tyburn Walk, St Sepulchre's Church EC4 to Hyde Park Corner
Widow's Bun Ceremony, Widow's Son, Devons Road E3

Northamptonshire
Broughton Tin Can Band, Broughton
Corby Pole Fair, Corby

Northumberland
Dunting the Freeholder, Newbiggin-by-the-Sea
Tar Barrels Parade, Allendale Town

Oxfordshire
Garland Dressing, Charlton-on-Otmoor
Lot-meadow Drawing, Yarnton
May Morning, Magdalen College, Oxford
Mayor of Ock Street, Abingdon

Rutland
Horse Shoe Tax, Oakham Castle, Oakham

Shropshire
Arbor Day, Aston-on-Clun

Somerset
Guy Fawkes Carnival, Bridgwater
Minehead Hobby Horse, Minehead
Wassailing the Apple Trees, Carhampton

Staffordshire
Abbots Bromley Horn Dance, Abbots Bromley
Greenhill Bower and Court of Array, Lichfield
Sheriff's Ride, Lichfield

Suffolk
Jankyn Smith's Charity, Bury St Edmunds

Surrey
Forty Shilling Day, Wotton, near Dorking

Sussex
Lewes Bonfire Night, Lewes
Ebernoe Horn Fair, near Petworth
Little Edith's Treat, Piddinghoe, near Lewes
Marbles Championship, Tinsley Green, near Crawley

The Thames
Swan Upping, River Thames from Sunbury to Pangbourne

Warwickshire
Cyclists' Memorial Service, Meriden
Grand Wardmote of the Woodmen of Arden, Meriden
Wroth Silver, Knightlow Hill, Ryton-on-Dunsmore

Wiltshire
Grovely Rights Day, Great Wishford
Midsummer Day Ritual, Stonehenge

Yorkshire
Burning Bartle, West Witton
Denby Dale Pie, Denby Dale
Hornblowing, Bainbridge
Hornblowing, Ripon
Kiplingcotes Derby, South Dalton
Maypole Raising, Barwick-in-Elmet
Penny Hedge, Whitby
St Wilfrid's Feast Procession, Ripon
Tolling the Devil's Knell, Dewsbury

Variable Locations
Royal Maundy – different cathedral annually
Welsh National Eisteddfod – different location annually

Abbots Bromley Horn Dance
Abbots Bromley, Staffordshire

*Monday following the first
Sunday after 4 September*

The Horn Dance at Abbots Bromley is one of the most celebrated annual customs or ceremonies rooted in a particular place. It commences at 8 o'clock in the morning, or shortly afterwards, on Wakes Monday, when the performers have collected the horns and their costumes from the parish church, where they have lain throughout the year.

There are twelve in the company, foremost being the six horn-dancers, who wear or carry the ancient sets of reindeer horns. The others are 'Maid Marian', a man dressed not as a maid but as a woman, and who carries a ladle for collecting money; a hobby-horse, a man or boy who wears a traditional costume, though his horse has snapping jaws; a boy with a bow and arrow; and a fool dressed in motley, with cap and bells. Then there are the two musicians, a man who plays the melodian for the dancers to dance by, and a boy with a triangle.

Though the costume of the dancers only dates back to those designed by the vicar's daughters in the latter half of the 19th century, the assembled company in their floppy hats have a truly medieval appearance – the mingled greens and browns harking back to the forest, where the dance is supposed to have originated.

The dance itself is not a complex affair, and after its initial performance the same pattern is repeated throughout the day. The dancers assemble in single file and, as the music commences, they break into a simple step. They weave in and out of each other before forming a ring, which breaks into a figure of eight. Then they separate into two facing lines, three horn-bearers each facing the other three. The two lines advance towards each other, the dancers lowering and raising their antlers in mock fight. They advance and retreat before passing through their opposing line to repeat the performance over again. They form a ring once more before filing off to the next venue. The horns are supported on the dancers' shoulders, the carved deer heads just beneath their chins. While the horn-bearers have challenged each other, Maid Marian has opposed the fool, and the boy-archer the hobby horse.

Having commenced near the church, the dancers make a tour of the parish, dancing outside houses, pubs and farms throughout the day, including a traditional performance outside Blithfield Hall, before returning to the church after an estimated tour of twenty miles. In the 19th century they were supposed to have covered more ground, but they took three or four days to do so.

Central to the mysterious origins of the dance itself are the horns. Curiously, they are not horns of a native deer, but of reindeer, a species extinct in Britain centuries before there are any records of the horn dance. The horns are mounted on a short pole on which has been set a carved deer's head. The heads have been painted over the years, but three are darker than the others, the darker set being known as 'the blue horns'. The widest of the horns are over three feet from tip to tip and weigh over 25 pounds.These are traditionally carried by the leader of the dance.

The horn dance has been in the hands of one of the local families for over four hundred years, it is claimed, and pride in their participation appears to have kept it that way. As to the history of the dance, it is first recorded in Robert Plot's *Natural History of Staffordshire* in 1686. The antiquarian describes a curious custom called the hobby-horse dance, which he says has been practised at 'Paget's Bromley' within memory of persons living when he wrote. On Twelfth Day a man carrying a hobby-horse used to dance in the street, holding in his hand a bow and arrow, and accompanied by six men carrying deers' heads on their shoulders.

'To this Hobby-horse dance,' he says, 'there also belonged a *pot*, which was kept in turnes by 4 or 5 of the *chief* of the *Town*, whom they call'd Reeves, who provided *Cakes* and *Ale* to put in the pot; all people who had any kindness for the good intent of the Institution of the *Sport*, giving pence a piece for themselves and families; and so *forraigners* too, that came to see it; with which mony (the charge of the Cakes and Ale being defrayed) they not only repaired their *church* but kept their *poore* too; which charges are not now perhaps so cheerfully boarn.'

The origins of the dance are a matter of conjecture, as well as why the original date was changed from Christmastide at Twelfth Day to the church's wakes in September. One theory is that as Abbots Bromley was on the edge of Needwood Forest and some of the early inhabitants were foresters, it is a celebration of a charter of 1125, which granted grazing rights in the forest to the villagers. Another, that it was possibly the dance of some foresters' guild. Perhaps Shakespeare got as close as possible in a song in *As You Like It*:

What shall he have that killeth the deer?
His leather skin and horns to wear.
　　Then sing him home.
Take thou no scorn to wear the horn!
It was a crest ere thou wast born;
　　Thy father's father wore it
　　And thy father bore it
The horn, the horn, the lusty horn
Is not a thing to laugh to scorn.

And whether Shakespeare composed the song or borrowed it from another must itself be conjecture. Whatever else, the Abbots Bromley Horn Dance is a remarkable survival of an ancient custom with all its vitality and its mystery intact.

Abbotsbury Garland Day

Abbotsbury, Dorset

13 May

Abbotsbury Garland Day is a survival from the days when the village had its own small fishing fleet. It takes place on Old May Day, which also coincided with the start of the fishing season and, in the days when fishing families had their own boats, they made garlands which they showed off round the village. There is some confusion as to whether the garlands were taken to the church for a service before they adorned the prows of their owners' boats and were then taken out to sea, or whether they were taken out to sea first and then returned for a blessing, though the former seems more likely.

The custom has been kept alive by the children of the village, who make two separate sets of garlands, one of wild flowers and one of flowers from the garden. These are taken round the village to be admired, the bell-shaped garlands carried on poles between two children, and donations are happily accepted for their pains.

An officious policeman tried to put an end to the custom in 1954, when he stopped the procession through the village and seized the money that the children had so far collected, claiming that it was no more than an excuse to go begging. The children's parents, after organising a procession of protest, took their complaint to the Chief Constable. The custom proved stronger than the petty officiousness of a village policeman, who it seems was transferred. That it lives on is a tribute to the independence of a small Dorset village, and a reminder that the inhabitants once harvested the sea.

Admiralty Court

Rochester, Kent

First or second Saturday in July

The Mayor of Rochester has, since the 15th century, also been known as the Admiral of Medway, and in this capacity he presides over the Admiralty Court of the City of Rochester. The colourful ceremony, with the dignitaries dressed in their official regalia, takes place on a decorated barge moored in the River Medway. The Court was set up by Act of Parliament in 1729 'for regulating, well-ordering, Governing and Improving the Oyster Fishery in the River Medway and waters thereof'. The Court consists of the aldermen of the City and a jury made up of freemen of the river, and its purpose is to swear in new water bailiffs and ordain the Medway's oyster fishery for the following year.

Antrobus Souling Play
Antrobus, Cheshire

*31 October and other nights
over next two weeks*

The Antrobus Souling Play is performed at the Antrobus Arms in Antrobus, and in various other pubs, from Hallowe'en onwards over the following two weeks. The company perform a souling, or mumming, play, to which they have added some touches of their own, including the Wild Horse and his Driver. The performers all dress up for their parts, which include King George, the Black Prince, the Quack Doctor, Mary, Beelzebub and Derry Doubt. The Wild Horse has a fearsome aspect and snapping jaws, and lines about him are recited to attract sympathy for his needy condition.

In the Middle Ages, prayers were said for souls suffering in purgatory on All Saints' and All Souls' Day at the beginning of November, and though the practice was swept aside at the Reformation, the poor still had a tradition of begging for soul-cakes in payment for prayers. Children kept up that custom in Shropshire and Cheshire singing 'Soul, soul, for a souling cake'. Souling plays, a variant of Christmas mumming plays, survived in Cheshire until after the Second World War. The Antrobus Souling Play is now the only one, and this version is one that was revived in the 1920s after it had lapsed for a brief time.

Appleby Horse Fair

Appleby, Cumbria

Week of second Wednesday in June

Appleby Horse Fair is the largest traditional horse fair of its kind still flourishing. It is also the largest annual gypsy gathering in the country, and takes place in early June, the focus being the big sale day on the second Wednesday of the month. For weeks beforehand the gypsies begin to arrive from all over the country, bringing their horses, ponies, caravans and trailers. There are harness races preceding the Wednesday sale day to enliven the proceedings, and an abundance of showmen and fairground hucksters to take advantage of the gathering.

The fair has taken place in early June since 1751, but before then an April Charter Fair was established in 1685. Certainly, many more people go to the fair than those who are interested in buying or selling horses.

Arbor Day

Aston-on-Clun, Shropshire

29 May

Once a year, a black poplar tree in the middle of the village of Aston-on-Clun is bedecked with flags. The flags are attached to long poles and they remain in place until the following year, when they are taken down and the flags are renewed by the villagers.

The custom has taken place on 29 May every year since late in the 1780s to commemorate the wedding of the local squire, John Marston, to his bride Mary Carter. It is uncertain whether the tree was traditionally dressed in this way before the squire's marriage, or whether the bride thought it had been done especially for her benefit. From the date of her wedding, however, she herself ordered new flags every year and left instructions to ensure the custom was continued after her death. In the 1950s the Marston family sold up its estates; the parish council agreed to take over the responsibility and has continued to observe the custom ever since.

A number of theories have been proffered to suggest that the tree was adorned in this way before the Marston marriage. One suggests that it was traditionally dressed before then on Oak Apple Day (the day of the wedding, by design or accident); another, that because at some stage the tree was called 'the bride's tree', that it was in honour of St Brigit, who lived a life of seclusion in the woods. Since St Brigit is the patron saint of poets, blacksmiths and healers, this seems fanciful. The custom does add a touch of colour to the village throughout the year, as it has done for more than two hundred years, and possibly a lot longer.

Sadly, in the late 1990s, the tree's demise has meant that the custom has been halted. However, efforts are being made to establish an alternative form of the ceremony.

Ashbourne Ball Game

Ashbourne, Derbyshire

Shrove Tuesday and Ash Wednesday

The Shrove Tuesday Ball Game at Ashbourne, now known as the
Royal Shrovetide Football Game, is one of the most famous ball games,
though there are others which claim a longer history, such as the one
at Atherstone in Warwickshire. The Ashbourne game takes place
between the Up'ards and Down'ards and starts at 2 o'clock in the
afternoon, when a specially prepared ball – slightly larger than a
football and filled with cork – is thrown in by a visiting guest of
honour. The goals are two mills some three miles apart, and the ball
may be kicked, carried or thrown, but generally proceeds in a series of
'hugs', invisible to the spectator. Often the ball is fought for in the
stream which runs through the pitch, and the game can last for many
hours, finishing after dark.

It was first recorded in 1682, though thought to be much older, and
various attempts were made to suppress it over the years. In 1891, it is
said, the police attempted to prevent the game from being started at
all, but the ball was smuggled in under the skirts of a woman. It has
continued unabated ever since, and by 1928 it had become so
respectable that the then Prince of Wales was invited to start the game
– hence the name Royal.

Other Shrove Tuesday games take place at Atherstone in Warwickshire
(as mentioned above); Sedgefield, Co Durham; also at Alnwick,
Northumberland, where the ball is piped into the field of play by the
Duke of Northumberland's piper. Other than at Shrovetide, there are
ball games at Workington in Cumbria on Good Friday, Easter Tuesday
and the following Saturday.

Baddeley Cake

Drury Lane Theatre, London

Twelfth Night

The Baddeley Cake is a fairly recent Twelfth Night custom and has been kept alive, appropriately enough by the theatrical profession, to honour the memory of one of their members. After the last performance on Twelfth Night, the cast of whatever play is currently being performed at the Drury Lane Theatre assembles to celebrate the name of Robert Baddeley by eating a slice of the Baddeley Cake and drinking his health in a glass of wine.

Robert Baddeley was a cook who became a successful actor at Drury Lane, and when he died in 1794, he not only left a considerable sum of money to the Drury Lane Theatre Fund – founded by David Garrick in 1766 for the relief of distressed members of the company – but also £100 to pay for a cake and wine, to be enjoyed by the cast playing on Twelfth Night, still in costume and after the last performance.

The custom has been carried on since 1794 except, naturally, when the theatre is dark, despite a gloomy account of its demise in Robert Chambers' *Book of Days*, published in the 1860s, in which he said:

'We have a Twelfth Night celebration recorded in theatrical history. Baddeley, the Comedian . . . left by will money to provide cake and wine for the performers in the Green Room at Drury Lane Theatre on Twelfth Night; but the bequest is not now observed in this manner.'

Robert Chambers is wrong, but the custom is a strictly private theatrical affair, and not one that can be witnessed by the general public.

Battle of Neville's Cross

Durham Cathedral

Saturday nearest 29 May

Every year, after evensong, on the Saturday nearest to 29 May, the choristers of Durham Cathedral climb up the central tower to sing anthems of thanksgiving. They sing from the north, the south and the east, but not the west.

This is in commemoration of the Battle of Neville's Cross, fought just outside the city on 17 October 1346, when the English defeated an invading Scots army led by King David II. Edward III was away in France besieging Calais, and it is said the French encouraged the Scots king to make a diversionary attack on England. The Northern nobles were rallied by Edward 's consort, Queen Phillippa, and the Scots were routed. The monks from the cathedral had played their part by making their way to Maiden's Bower, a hill near the Scots lines, and placing a spear there with the sacred cloth of St Cuthbert held aloft. They prayed for victory and the Abbot vowed annual masses from the cathedral tower. After the Restoration, the date of the ceremony was changed to 29 May, and the choristers have continued the custom originally undertaken by the monks. The reason the anthem isn't also sung from the western side of the tower, it is said, is because once when it was being sung from there, a chorister fell to his death; it was discontinued either as a mark of respect or because of the possible danger.

There are other suggestions as to the origins of the commemoration; one that it was the conclusion of the great guilds procession that took place on 29 May; another that it celebrates the extinguishing of the fire of 25 May 1429, which spared the cathedral but burnt down the tower.

Bawming the Thorn
Appleton, near Warrington, Cheshire
Third Saturday in June

The custom of 'bawming the thorn' is carried out by the children of Appleton in the middle of the village, where the thorn tree stands inside a railed enclosure. After a procession through the village, the children 'bawm' (adorn) the hawthorn tree with garlands, ribbons and flags. They then dance round the tree in a ring, singing a traditional song. This is followed by children's sports and a festival tea for all concerned.

The original tree was supposed to have been an offshoot of the Holy Thorn of Glastonbury planted by Adam de Dutton in 1125, although the present tree dates from only 1967, replacing the previous one that died in 1965. It has been suggested that the custom harks back to a memory of pre-Christian tree worship, the hawthorn (also known as the whitethorn or May-tree) having magical properties.

Certainly, it is an ancient custom, though the present revival dates back to the 1930s, after a previous revival at the turn of the century. At one time it was a well-known rural fête, with people coming from miles around, to such an extent that it was temporarily discontinued because of the trouble caused by the boisterous outsiders. Its survival as a custom in the hands of the village children suggests that its trouble-free continuance is assured.

Biddenden Dole, or Maids' Charity

Biddenden, Kent

Easter Monday

On Easter Monday in Biddenden, the pensioners and widows of the parish assemble outside a window of the old workhouse (now a dwelling) to collect their portion of the Biddenden Dole; a loaf of bread, a pound of cheese and a pound of tea. They also receive, as do curious visitors, a Biddenden Cake. This is, in fact, a biscuit stamped with the figures of two ladies, supposedly the twin sisters Eliza and Mary Chulkhurst, who it is claimed were joined at birth like Siamese twins at the shoulder and the hip. Their interlocked image on the biscuit is supposed to lend credence to this, as do the numbers on their aprons – one reading '34' and the other 'in 1100' – to the legend that they were born in 1100 and died thirty-four years later. One died before the other, the story has it, but though the survivor was offered her chance of a surgical separation, she declined and died a few hours later, having said 'As we came together, we will go together'. The Chulkhurst twins are supposed to have left their property to the poor of Biddenden, twenty acres of land still known as 'the Bread and Cheese Lands', the profits from which were to provide the annual dole – or charity – of bread, cheese and ale, and on which the old workhouse cottages now stand.

The source of the story was a locally published broadsheet in the early 1700s, but the historian Edward Hasted dismissed this in his *History and Antiquities of the County of Kent* in 1790. His claim was that the figures were not the Chulkhurst twins but 'two maidens of the name of Preston', to whom the land belonged and who were the real benefactors. Others say that the figures were neither pair of ladies but two of the recipients, poor widows of the parish. What is certain is that the charity was well-established by 1646 when the vicar, William Horner, attempted and failed to get the benefit from the Bread and Cheese Lands; ten years later, he tried and failed again.

Originally, the bread, cheese and ale were distributed inside the church on Easter Sunday, but this seems to have led to some disorder, as we discover in 1682 when Hinton, the then vicar, complained to the

Archbishop of Canterbury that the ale caused the custom 'to be observed with much disorder and indecency'. The ale was banished from the ceremony, to be replaced at a later date with tea, and the ceremony itself was banished to the church porch before it found its present home in the old workhouse. Standing on the Bread and Cheese Lands, this has now been converted into cottages, but the dole is still disbursed there thanks to an ancient charity that has survived down to the present day, keeping alive the memory of the Biddenden Maids, whoever they were.

Blessing the Throats
St Ethelreda, Ely Place, London ECI
3 February

On the feast of St Blaise at a Roman Catholic church in Ely Place, the service of Blessing the Throats takes place, where supplicants with afflictions of the throat receive a blessing before the altar. In the ceremony, a pair of candles which have been blessed are tied together with a ribbon at one end. These are lighted and the candles in a 'v' shape are placed on either side of the sufferer's throat while the priest recites the blessing: 'May the Lord deliver you from the evil of the throat and from every other evil.'

The ceremony has been performed here for over a century, though it is common in Catholic churches on the Continent. St Blaise was thought to have been the Bishop of Sebaste in Armenia and to have been put to death in the 4th century. The story goes that he was the son of rich and noble Christians, and was consecrated when very young. While he was in hiding in a cave, a woman brought him her son, who was on the point of death with a wishbone stuck in his throat, and whom he cured. Later, when he was imprisoned, the same woman brought him food and candles, and it was these that led to the blessing of St Blaise as described above. It is said that he was torn with wool-combs before being beheaded, and consequently became the patron of wool-combers. Parson Woodforde described a solemn procession in his honour at Norwich in 1783, and into the beginning of the 19th century St Blaise's Day was a general holiday in the wool towns of England and Scotland.

Bonfire Night

Ottery St Mary, Devon

5 November

They commemorate Guy Fawkes in Ottery St Mary with a day-long festival of fire and explosion. Early in the morning, the men fire off their homemade 'rock-cannons', as they do later in the day, at lunchtime and in the afternoon. The so-called 'tar-barrel rolling' is the climax to the day's festivities. Eighteen huge barrels, the insides especially coated in bitumen and primed with paraffin, are lit in turn and carried through the streets on men's shoulders, with sacking 'gloves' on their hands as their only protection. They charge through the streets until unable to stand the heat, and pass the barrel on to another. The bearing of the flaming tar-barrels for the grown-ups begins at about 7 o'clock in the evening, and the last one is finally dropped and rolled into the square about midnight. To cheers and singing, the tar-barrellers tear off their gloves and hurl them into the flames.

It is said that the flaming tar-barrellers were introduced to celebrate the landing of William III on 5 November 1688 at Torbay, though the origins of the rock-cannons are unknown. What *is* known is that various attempts were made to stop their use, both as unlawful and because they were dangerous, and that they now officially supervised and all the weapons are regularly checked.

Bread and Cheese Throwing

St Briavels, Gloucestershire

Whit Sunday evening

Following evensong on Whit Monday, basketfuls of bread and cheese are thrown from a wall near the old church, to be scrambled for in a lane below. This now fairly tame custom is thought to be the lone survivor of a number of such scrambles up and down the country.

St Briavels is the ancient capital of the Forest of Dean, and the ceremony is thought to have originated in the reign of King John, early in the 13th century. Its performance is thought to preserve the commoners' rights to grazing in the forest and cutting timber in nearby Hudnalls Wood. This right was documented in 1282 and upheld by Parliament in 1667, though its relation to the bread-and-cheese ceremony is unclear.

The custom itself was first recorded in 1779, when every householder had to pay a penny towards the cost of the bread and cheese. At that time the ceremony took place in the church itself, the bread and cheese being thrown to the congregation from above. It is recorded, however, that this caused 'as great a tumult and uproar as the amusements of a village wake', and the parson himself came under fire from pellets fashioned out of the bread and cheese. The ceremony was banished to the churchyard, the bread and cheese being thrown from the church tower, but this practice also fell into disrepute, as 'all the roughs of the Forest came over, and there was much drinking and fighting'. The present site for this well-established foresters' gathering is well away from the church, and pieces of bread and cheese are preserved by some of the locals who think they are blessed with good luck.

Britannia Coconut Dancers
Bacup, Lancashire

Easter Saturday

The Britannia Coconut Dancers are a strangely dressed group of eight unusual morris dancers whose formation is inextricably linked to their industrial background. On Easter Saturday they dance all day, starting in the village of Britannia at about 9 o'clock in the morning, dancing down into the middle of Bacup by midday, and then out of the town towards Stacksteads on the other side by the evening. Their processional dance leads from place to place, and they have a number of other dances, some with garlands and others in which they strike their 'coconuts' together, worn at the waist, the knee and on the palms of the hands. These 'nuts' are in fact mahogany blocks to represent the old bobbin-tops from the cotton mills, and from whence is derived part of their name. Their costume, like their faces, is predominantly black: black jerseys, knee-breeches and clogs, though they have white socks, short skirts and headgear, on which is pinned a large rosette.

The team was founded in 1857 at the Royal Britannia Cotton Mills, and the dancers were described in a newspaper in 1908 as belonging to the 'cocoa-nutters Morris Dance'. Presumably the coconut comes from the sound of the bobbin-tops clicking together, much as do castanets.

Broughton Tin Can Band
Broughton, Northamptonshire

Second Sunday in December

For those who've ever wondered what a charivari is (part of the famous subtitle to the magazine *Punch*), they can witness one in action in Broughton, Northants, on a cold night in December. The Broughton Tin Can Band assembles near the parish church of St Andrew, and at midnight the members all begin to beat cans, saucepan lids and anything else that makes an unpleasant noise before setting off to do their unmusical tour of the village.

It is not known how, why or when the custom began, nor why it is kept up, despite attempts to suppress it, but the feeling is that it shouldn't be allowed to lapse. There are two theories offered as to what may have started it: one, that it was used to frighten away gypsies who'd set up a camp nearby, unlikely though this may sound; the other is that it is a hangover from a celebration on the eve of the village feast of St Andrew, before the calendar change of 1752 when it was decreed that 1st January should be the first day of 1752 and that 2nd September 1752 should be followed by 14th September. A charivari, according to the dictionary, is 'a medley of sounds, hubbub; a serenade of pans and trays to an unpopular person'.

Burning Bartle

West Witton, Yorkshire

Saturday nearest 24 August

In the Wensleydale village of West Witton, on the Saturday nearest to St Bartholomew's Day, the patron saint, the ritual Burning of Bartle takes place. Bartle is a slightly more than life-size effigy of a man, constructed with combustible materials and with flashing eyes. At 9pm, he is carried on a tour of the village before meeting his fiery end. He pauses outside pubs and houses, particularly those of the elderly inhabitants, and wherever he does so, his chant is taken up:

> *At Penhill Crags he tore his rags,*
> *At Hunter's Thorn he blew his horn,*
> *At Capplebank Stee, he brak his knee,*
> *At Grassgill Beck he brak his neck,*
> *At Waddam's End he couldn't fend*
> *At Grassgill End we'll mak his end.*

And to the cry of 'Shout, boys, shout!', the crowd gives a loud cheer, many of them raising a drink to their lips, before moving on to the next halting place.

When Bartle and his retinue reach the foot of the village – Grassgill End – he is ritually stabbed with a knife before being ignited, to the delight of all. As the fire blazes, the assembled company breaks out singing, though there is no traditional song associated with the custom.

The popular version of the origins of Burning Bartle is that he was a notorious pig thief who lived on Penhill hundreds of years ago. The men of the village of West Witton decided to put a stop to his knavery, and set out to capture him. They chased him all over hill and dale – including those named in the chant, such as Capplebank Stee and Grassgill Beck – before they trapped him at Grassgill End where he was slain.

Another version has it that he was the wicked Giant of Penhill, with a herd of prize pigs, and was killed by local farmers – his fate to lie on the hill 'in a grave big enough for ten'.

Yet another sees in the name of Bartle in association with St Bartholomew, whose day, or near enough, is used to mark the custom. It is thought that before the Reformation there would have been an effigy in the church of St Bartholomew and that this might have been removed by the parishioners to save him from desecration. In the attempt, they were pursued and the effigy was damaged as in the chant, until it was seized at Grassgill End and burnt.

A trust fund was set up in the village comparatively recently to ensure Burning Bartle's survival, though it would seem hardly necessary with such a custom so obviously honoured and enjoyed by the village.

Cheese Rolling
Cooper's Hill, Brockworth, Gloucestershire
Spring Bank Holiday Monday

The Cheese Rolling at Cooper's Hill is one of the most spectacular and hazardous of rural English customs. It takes place at about 6 o'clock in the evening on an extremely steep hill and is open to all. A Master of Ceremonies, wearing a white coat and a festively beribboned top hat, is in attendance to see the competitors get off to a fair start. On the count of three, the first cheese is rolled, and on 'four' the competitors launch themselves in pursuit. Inevitably, the wheel-shaped cheese reaches the bottom before it is seized, so the winner is the one to arrive immediately afterwards.

There are a number of cheeses rolled, depending on how many have been donated, and one specifically for girls. The cheeses are traditionally Double Gloucesters, as is befitting, and the honour of rolling them is given to specially invited guests. At the top of the hill is a permanent maypole marking the starting place, and the hill is thickly wooded save for a wide strip where the cheese rolling takes place.

The custom was traditionally held on Whit Monday and was one of a number of other events, all part of a well-known local wake. There is a notice dating back to 1836 announcing that there were 'two cheeses to be run for' and among other competitions there was 'chattering for a bladder of snuff by old women', 'jumping the bag' and 'grinning for the cake' – presumably a gurning competition. At some stage late in the last century, the wake seems to have been largely suppressed as being too rowdy, only the cheese rolling surviving until today. It was continued throughout the last war, and during rationing dummies were used, bearing a token piece of cheese inside.

There are various theories on offer as to the history of the custom, a truly fanciful one suggesting that it was introduced by Phoenician traders in honour of Baal, as a kind of sun worship. More likely, and more acceptable locally, is that it was a ceremony of record, to perpetuate certain rights, akin to beating the bounds.

Clipping the Church
St Mary's, Painswick, Gloucestershire
19 September (or nearest Sunday)

On the Sunday of the Feast of the Nativity of St Mary (old-style), at St Mary's Church at Painswick, the ceremony of clipping the church takes place. This happens in the afternoon when the children of the village encircle the church holding hands. Singing a special hymn, they advance on the church and retreat from it three times, dressed especially for the occasion, the boys with buttonholes and the girls each wearing a flower in their hair. Thereafter, a special sermon is preached in the open air, from the door of the belfry. The children are rewarded with a bun each, along with a modest coin.

Clipping the Church was part of the Feast that dates back for centuries, and was revived by the vicar, the Rev W. H. Seddon, in the latter part of the last century. He wrote a pamphlet called *Painswick Feast*, where he said that though the feast was very much alive, 'the "clipping" of the church had been intermittent for some years. Many of the old people in the village, however, well remembered taking part in it in the days of their youth, and both name and custom were revived from their lips.'

Another custom associated with the Feast is the baking of Puppy-dog Pies, small cakes containing little china dogs. The vicar associated these with the ancient Roman feast of *Lupercalia*, though local wisdom has it that a greedy publican, eager to profit from crowds attending the Feast, used a litter of puppies to augment the filling of his meat pies. The feast was at one time notorious for both its riotous behaviour and for its suspicious meat pies.

Colchester Oyster Ceremony
Colchester, Essex
1 September

There is a civic ceremony to open the oyster season in Colchester which takes place every year on 1 September, in a tradition dating back almost a thousand years. The mayor, the town clerk and members of the council, along with members of the Fishery Board, embark from Brightlingsea in a fishing boat for the oyster beds in Pyefleet Creek. Here the clerk, in robes of office, reads the ancient proclamation of 1256. This declares that the fishing rights in the River Colne 'from time beyond which memory runneth not to the contrary' belong and appertain to the Corporation of the Borough of Colchester. After a loyal toast is drunk, pieces of gingerbread are eaten and glasses of gin are swallowed. The mayor, in full regalia, then lowers the trawl to dredge up the first oysters of the season, one of which by tradition he must swallow himself.

Colchester oysters were famous even before Roman times, and it was Richard I in 1156 who bestowed the Colne Fishing Rights on the Borough of Colchester. There used to be a magnificent civic Oyster Feast towards the end of October, but the extravagance of this was curtailed by the Municipal Reform Act of 1835. The tradition is carried on today, somewhat abated, and takes place in the Moot Hall on or around 20 October.

Common Walk

Laugharne, Dyfed

Spring Bank Holiday Monday
(every three years: 1999, 2002 etc)

Every three years, early in the morning on the Spring Bank Holiday in Laugharne, the people are summoned by the bailiff ringing the Town Hall bell. This is a signal for them to assemble for the Common Walk, led by the Portreeve and covering nearly 25 miles. Among the officers are halberdiers, mattock-men, flag-bearers and guides. En route are twenty-six places where the mattock-men mark their passing. At any one of these places, officials have the right to challenge any of the walkers to name the place correctly, such as Chief Hill or Beggar's Bush, each one having its own name peculiar to the place. Those who don't know the name are liable to be hoisted upside down and beaten three times with a staff.

Laugharne is administered by a corporation headed by a Portreeve, who presides over a Court Leet and Court Baron, under a charter granted by Sir Gwydo de Brione in 1307. The Common Walk honours one of the conditions of the charter, and preserves the rights and privileges to certain land-tenures granted to the seventy-six burgesses. Those eligible to be burgesses must be over 21 years old, have lived in Laugharne a year, or have acquired their status by being sons or sons-in-law of burgesess.

Dylan Thomas lived in the Boat House and was buried in Laugharne. It is not recorded whether he ever took part in the Common Walk.

Cotswold Olympic Games
Chipping Campden, Gloucestershire
Friday and Saturday following Spring Bank Holiday

The proudly-named Cotswold Olympic Games take place on Dover's Hill outside Chipping Campden, though they are only a vestigial survival of a once majestic sporting occasion. Today, you might expect to see a display of Scottish dancing, a tug of war and climbing the greasy pole, as well as such modern innovations as a motorcycle display.

The event was founded in 1605 as 'Mr Robert Dover's Olimpick Games upon the Cotswold Hills', the ebullient founder having obtained permission from James I to hold an annual Whitsun 'Olimpick Games', designed for 'harmless mirth and jollitie'.

The games opened with the firing of a gun mounted on a wooden castle, which was erected on the summit of a hill. This was billed as 'the famous and admirable portable Fabricke of Dover Castle, her Ordnance and Artillery'. In the early days you could expect to enjoy cudgel playing, skittles, pitching the bar, leaping, wrestling, football, hunting the hare (which was not to be killed), leap-frog, walking on hands, jumping in sacks, cock-fighting, horse-racing over a mile course, backsword-play, handling the pike and, for the non-squeamish, a shin-kicking contest. In 1652 an anthology of 308 poems in praise of the games was published under the title of *Annalia Dubrensia*.

Over the years, the games became rowdier and rowdier, until the earlier part of the 19th century when the 'scum and refuse of the nearest factory towns' converged in their thousands on Chipping Campden and, it is said, 'armed bands of Birmingham yahoos swilled unlimited beer from unlimited booths'. The games were suppressed in 1852 and almost forgotten. They were revived at the time of the Festival of Britain in 1951, and have continued more genteelly ever since.

On the day following the Cotswold Olympics, the traditional Saturday Scuttlebrooke Wake takes place in Chipping Campden. This has its carnival queen and fancy-dress parade with dancing in the town square.

Dicing for Bibles

St Ives, Cambridgeshire

Whit Monday

On or about Whit Monday, in the parish church of St Ives, twelve local children – six boys and six girls – play dice for the possession of six new bibles. Churchwardens keep the score and the vicar supervises the proceedings, which are usually watched by the mayor and mayoress. The game is preceded by a short address, the Lord's Prayer and a hymn.

This quaint custom came about at the bequest of Dr Robert Wilde in his will of 1675 when he instructed that: '£50 be laid out on a piece of land as would so produce a rental of £3 p.a., to be expended in bibles and paid into the hands of the Vicar and Churchwardens. An annual sermon is forever to be preached in the parish church on "the Excellency, Perfection and Divine Authority of the Scriptures". The Minister shall give notice when the sermon shall be preached and twelve children, six male and six female, shall cast dice for six bibles. The Minister shall kneel and pray God "to direct the lots of His glory" and receive 10 shillings, the clerk 12 pence. Such money remaining shall be expended by the vicar and churchwarden on a comfortable dinner for themselves, with as much claret and sack as the remaining money will provide.'

The bibles have been diced for ever since, though the dinner, claret and sack have somehow fallen by the wayside. And the land itself, which was purchased from the £50, and which became known as the Bible Orchard, was sold to provide for a new library which now stands upon it, though preserving sufficient for an investment to enable the custom to continue.

The ceremony has not always taken place in the church, however. In 1880 the bishop of the diocese thought that the communion table was not the right place for such an activity, and a table was set up by the chancel steps. Later the custom was moved out of the church altogether, to the church school, though it has now been restored to its rightful place in the church.

Doggett's Coat and Badge Race

Between London and Chelsea Bridges
1 August or nearest date, depending on tides

On or about 1 August, depending on the tides, six London watermen compete for the Doggett's Coat and Badge by sculling up the Thames from London to Chelsea Bridge. The race commences at 11 o'clock and is started by the Worshipful Company of Fishmongers' Bargemaster. The skiffs have to cover nearly five miles, negotiating a number of bridges, and are followed by a flotilla of boats bearing representatives of fishmongers, watermen and lightermen. The date is chosen so that the entrants can row with the tide.

Founded in 1715, it is claimed to be the oldest continuously contested boat race, albeit that it was suspended during the First and Second World Wars. The missing five years of the First were rowed consecutively in 1920 and those of the Second in 1947. Thomas Doggett, the founder of the race, was an Irish actor, and manager in turn of both the Haymarket and the Drury Lane theatres.

He chose to inaugurate the race in theatrical style with notices posted on the walls of London, which read:

> 'This being the day of His Majesty's happy Accession to the Throne, there will be given by Mr Doggett an Orange Livery with a Badge representing Liberty to be rowed for by Six Watermen that are out of their time within the year past. They are to row from London Bridge to Chelsea. It will continue annually on the same day forever.'

He died in 1721 and left money to 'continue the custom'. The executors approached the Fishmongers' Company, asking them 'to take the execution of the said Trust upon them in consideration of the sum of £300' and, in conjunction with the Company of Watermen, they have supervised the race ever since.

It is said that Thomas Doggett had been truly impressed by a young oarsman who rowed him home to Chelsea one stormy night and this, coupled with his enthusiasm for the House of Hanover after he had been commanded to appear before George I, was the inspiration of the Coat and Badge Race.

The race was confined to six watermen 'out of their time within the year past', that is, those who have finished their apprenticeship in the preceding year. The watermen, or wherrymen, were at that time as important for getting about London as taxi drivers are today. Originally, the race was *against* the tide and took four or five hours to complete, as opposed to the twenty-five or thirty minutes today; also, the boats were much heavier and much more ungainly. The race originally began at the Old Swan at London Bridge and finished at the Old Swan at Chelsea. The winner was awarded an orange coat with accompanying breeches, cap, stockings and buckle shoes, as well as a large shield bearing the white horse of Hanover with the legend 'Liberty', which is worn on the left arm. Today both pubs have vanished and the coat is scarlet as opposed to orange.

The winner is presented to the Prime Warden of the Company of Fishmongers at their annual dinner at Fishmongers' Hall in November. He is thereafter expected to be available to escort the Prime Warden on formal occasions, to accompany the Queen on the Royal Barge, to march in the Lord Mayor's Show and to help oversee the succeeding races. Of course, since he is one of many, he is not necessarily called upon to fulfil all these obligations in any one year.

Dunmow Flitch Trials

Great Dunmow, Essex

June every leap year

The Dunmow Flitch trials take place every leap year, when intrepid couples who claim to be happily married submit themselves for a trial, at the end of which, if their case is proved, they become the proud possessors of a Dunmow Flitch of bacon. The jury is made up of 'six maidens and six bachelors of Dunmow', and the trial is presided over by a judge with counsels both for the claimants and 'for the bacon'. A number of couples may stand trial, though they have to satisfy a committee before being selected. If the jury find 'for the bacon', the unsuccessful claimants go away empty-handed and presumably spend the rest of their married life rowing about it.

The Dunmow Flitch has a long and illustrious history, being alluded to by two great 14th-century poets: William Langland, in *Piers Plowman*, who averred that joyless couples would never win 'the flicche of Donemow', and Geoffrey Chaucer in *The Canterbury Tales* with the lines:

> *The bacoun was nat feet for hem, I trowe,*
> *That some men han in Essex at Dunmowe.*

It is thought to have originated some time in the 13th century, with a gift of land by a Robert Fitzwalter to the priory at Little Dunmow, a condition of which was that a flitch of bacon was to be presented to any man prepared to state publicly and on oath before the Prior and the people of the entire village that he had never rued giving up his bachelorhood for a year and a day. The first record of the presentation is in 1445, when it was won by a Richard Wright, and there are records again in 1467 and 1510. In 1640, after the Reformation, it was mentioned as a thing of the past, and it was not until 1701 that it was revived, when William and Jane Parsley, and another couple, each received a flitch and were made to swear on oath that:

> *You shall swear by custom and confession*
> *If ever you made nuptial transgression*
> *Be you either married man or wife*

If you have brawls or contentious strife;
Or otherwise at bed or board
Offended each other in deed or word;
Or since the parish clerk said Amen
You wished yourself unmarried again;
Or in a twelvemonth and a day
Repented not in thought in any way;
But continued true in thought and desire
As when you joined hands in the quire;
If these conditions without all fear
Or your own accord you will freely swear
A whole gammon of bacon you shall receive
And bear it hence with love and good leave:
For this is our custom at Dunmow well known
Though the pleasure be ours, the bacon's your own.

There is a record of an award in 1751, when the flitch was given to Thomas and Ann Shakeshaft, but such was the attendant high spirits of a large crowd that Little Dunmow declined to honour the custom thereafter, save to offer a flitch to Queen Victoria and her consort in 1841, when it was politely declined.

It was revived in 1885, in Great Dunmow, by the novelist Harrison Ainsworth. He wrote a historical novel called *The Flitch of Bacon* and then donated two flitches himself, thus ensuring publicity for his book and the recommencement of the custom.

Dunting the Freeholder
Newbiggin-by-the-Sea, Northumberland
Wednesday nearest 18 May

Once a year the freeholders of Newbiggin-by-the-Sea do a perambulation of the bounds, in the course of which the 'dunting' of a new freeholder takes place, that is if there is a new one to be dunted. In the ceremony, the freeholder is lifted by the feet and shoulders, and his or her backside is dunted gently against the dunting stone. The Secretary of the Freeholders meanwhile proclaims that this or that person is 'this day admitted a member of the ancient body of freeholders'.

This boundary-marking perambulation has taken place at Newbiggin since 1235, and no freeholder is entitled to call himself one until he has been dunted in the traditional manner. There are sixty freeholders, many of whom have acquired their status by inheritance, though it is possible to become one by buying a house to which the entitlement is attached.

Dunting the freeholder is peculiar to Newbiggin, though the perambulation is traditional, in common with many other beating the bounds customs up and down the country. Until recently, nuts and raisins were scattered during the perambulation, to be scrambled for by children.

Durham Miners' Gala

Durham

Second Saturday in July

The Durham Miners' Gala is an echo of what was once one of the largest annual trade union gatherings in Europe. Miners from the various Durham lodges, as well as representatives from other areas, march behind their bands and elaborately-worked banners, from the outskirts of the city to the old race-track by the River Wear. Here they are addressed by prominent miners' leaders and Labour politicians.

It began in 1871 as a demonstration of solidarity by the newly-formed Durham Miners' Union and, during its heyday, it used to attract a quarter of a million people – miners and their families, as well as fraternal delegates. Nowadays it is only a reminder of the massive army of men who once toiled underground to bring up coal. Pit-closures in recent years have reduced the workforce to a fraction of its former strength. Nevertheless, the Gala Day is still an occasion for a gathering of Durham miners and their families, for political speeches and for the fun of the fair.

Ebernoe Horn Fair

Ebernoe, near Petworth, Sussex

25 July

The two traditional events that take place at Ebernoe Horn Fair are the roasting of a horned sheep or ram and a cricket match between the village and one of its neighbours. The horns of the sheep are carefully preserved, and duly presented to the highest scorer of the winning side at the end of the day.

It is claimed that the custom goes back many centuries, though presumably the winner of some contest other than cricket took the horns as a prize, and it was revived in its present form in 1864. There is a local ballad about the fair which suggests there might originally have been some kind of horn dance associated with it, or possibly it was a warning to complacent husbands:

> *If you would see Horn Fair you must walk on your way*
> *I will not let you ride on my grey mare today*
> *You'd rumple all my muslin and uncurl my hair*
> *And leave me all distressed to be seen at Horn Fair.*
>
> *Oh, fairest of damsels, how can you say No?*
> *With you I intend to Horn Fair for to go*
> *We'll join the finest company when we do go there*
> *With horns on their heads, boys, the finest of the fair.*

Egremont Crab Fair

Egremont, Cumbria

Saturday nearest 18 September

Egremont Crab Fair often known as 'Crabapple Fair' is exceptional for an event that takes place nowhere else. This is the World Gurning Championship, one of the many sporting events on offer throughout the day. The fair commences at dawn, when a greasy pole is erected, on top of which is placed a prize, which can be of food, such as a leg of lamb, or cash. There is an Applecart Parade, when apples are thrown from the back of a lorry and are scrambled for by youngsters, and many other sporting events associated with the area. There are street races, as well as a proper athletics meeting, hound trails, Cumberland and Westmorland wrestling and a terrier show. In the evening, the unusual events occur, such as competitions for best sentimental song-singer, the best junior joke-teller, the fastest clay-pipe smoker – all culminating in the Gurning Championship of the World. This has to be done through a horse-collar, called 'gurnin' through a braffin', and one is specially kept for the purpose. Gurning, quite simply, is making the most horrible facial expression imaginable.

Egremont was granted a charter to hold a fair in 1267, though why it became known as the crab fair, or 't'crab', is not known. It is thought that at one time crab apples were distributed, instead of the more palatable ones used today, and that it celebrated the right of the local people to collect them – though since they grow wild and are free for anyone to pick, this seems fanciful. Another suggestion is that the Lord of the Manor, whose custom it was to attend the fair, distributed crab apples among the commonality. As to the gurning, it is certain that anyone biting a crab apple would make much the same expression as those you can see on the faces of the contestants in the gurning championship.

Eyam Plague Memorial

Eyam, Derbyshire

Last Sunday in August

On the last Sunday in August in the village of Eyam in Derbyshire, there is a sombre but uplifting open-air church service. It takes place in the afternoon, when a procession leaves the church for a hilly and secluded spot outside the village called Cucklet Delph. The procession is led by the vicar, with a visiting nonconformist clergyman, the choir, a band and hundreds of worshippers. A commemoration service is held for those who died in the plague of 1665 and for the brave souls of those who survived in the cordoned-off village, which cut itself off entirely from the outside world for thirteen months.

When London was in the grip of the Great Plague of 1665, a bale of cloth was sent from there to an Eyam tailor called George Viccars. It is thought that fleas lodged in the cloth were responsible for passing on the plague to Viccars and his family, and shortly afterwards to other villagers. William Mompesson, the vicar, realised what was happening. In a courageous attempt to stop the spread of the plague elsewhere, he persuaded the villagers not to flee but to remain in the village, as he would, alongside them, until it had done its worst. The villagers agreed, and the vicar was able to organise that provisions of foodstuffs and other necessaries were left at the parish boundary for collection – payment for which, it is said, was left in a tray of vinegar. Not one of the seventy-six families survived untouched, and at the end of the day, some 250 of the village population of 350 had died, including the vicar's wife Catherine. It is thought that the heroism of the people of Eyam, following the example of their vicar William Mompesson, saved the rightly dreaded disease from spreading any further in the county. In his attempt to stop the spread of the plague in Eyam itself, Mompesson ceased to conduct services in the confined space of the church and held them outside in Cucklet Delph, where the memorial service takes place today.

Firing the Poppers

Fenny Stratford, Buckinghamshire

11 November

A noisy and explosive custom commemorates the building of St Martin's Church at Fenny Stratford. At noon on St Martin's Day, six small cannon, or Fenny Poppers, are fired off in turn, ignited with a red-hot iron rod. The first is fired by the vicar, the others by the verger, churchwardens and invited guests. The poppers are subsequently fired again at 2 o'clock and at 4 o'clock. The cannonade takes place in the local recreation ground adjoining the graveyard and has yet, as far as is known, to wake the dead.

It celebrates the building of Fenny Stratford's first parish church in 1730, which was brought about by the generosity and enthusiasm of the Lord of the Manor, Dr Browne Willis; he contributed most of the funds himself, but he also raised money from the local gentry by selling them space on the church's ceiling to display their coats of arms. He dedicated the church to the memory of his grandfather, from whom he had inherited the manor, and who died in St Martin's Lane, London, on St Martin's Day 1675. When Dr Willis died in 1760, he left money for a celebration of Martinmas, to provide for a sermon, a parish dinner and an entertainment. From thenceforward the Fenny Poppers have been fired on St Martin's Day, as well as a very few special occasions, such as the opening of the Grand Union Canal, Queen Victoria's Jubilee and the ending of the Second World War.

The poppers themselves are small cast-iron firing chambers, such as are used in large cannon, and date back to 1859, when they replaced the originals. It is the verger who has the task of priming the poppers, earning for himself the sobriquet of Master Gunner for the day.

Forty Shilling Day

Wotton, near Dorking, Surrey

2 February, though subject to alteration

Five clever and intrepid boys under the age of sixteen who are willing to brave the weather of a cold churchyard at Wotton in February, and who have retentive memories, can earn themselves 40 shillings each under the terms of William Glanville's will. To do so, they have to stand with both hands on his tombstone, recite the Lord's Prayer, the Apostles' Creed and the Ten Commandments. Next, they have to read aloud the fifteenth chapter of the First Epistle of St Paul to the Corinthians, and follow this by writing two verses of the Epistle in a clear and legible hand.

In 1717, when William Glanville made his will, 40 shillings was a considerable sum of money, but by choosing to die on 2 February (the date of his death being the day in which the commemorative service was to take place), he made it more difficult for the bequest to be honoured than if he had died in a milder month. The weather has not always been conducive to such an outdoor ceremony: on some occasions it has been postponed and on others a makeshift tent has been erected over the grave. If five boys can't be found from Wotton, neighbouring parishes are entitled to make up the numbers.

Garland Day

Castleton, Derbyshire

29 May (or preceding, if a Sunday)

On Oak Apple Day in Castleton in the Peak District, surrounded by the Blue John Caves, there is a delightful floral custom that takes over the whole village. After much preparation beginning very early in the morning with the making of a garland, the Garland King, mounted on a white horse and dressed in Stuart costume, is settled into a large, cone-shaped construction profusely decorated with flowers. On top of this is inserted another posy of flowers called 'the Queen'. Little is then visible of the King but a pair of legs on either side of his mount. He is accompanied or followed by his Lady, also mounted on a horse, though very much a lesser figure. The ceremony begins in the evening at one of the six village pubs that take in turn the honour of being the host. The procession is led round the village, the King and his Lady followed by the band and a flurry of white-clad girls bearing flowers. They stop at each of the pubs in turn for refreshments, where the girls dance a traditional air.

Having toured the village, the Garland King and his Lady ride to the church, where the Queen posy is removed from the King's Garland; the garland is then hauled to the top of the church to rest on one of the pinnacles, alongside the others which have been previously decorated with oak boughs. The King and his Lady return to the village green, where the girls do a traditional maypole dance. The King places the queen-posy on the War Memorial and the Last Post is sounded. Thereafter, the participants repair to the host pub, accompanied on their way by the dancing girls.

It would seem that this was one of the many May Day customs transferred to Oak Apple Day, in honour of the restoration of King Charles II, which might suggest why the King and his Lady are dressed in Stuart costume. At one stage, however, it is known that the King wore a red huntsman's coat – it can be seen in the local museum – which suggests that the costume has varied over the years.

Until about the mid-1950s the King's lady was in fact a man dressed as a woman, and up until the end of the last century, the dancers were not young girls but the bellringers, with oak-sprays in their hands. There are many strands in the custom that hark back to an earlier pre-Christian age. The oak motif is naturally associated with Druid customs, and the King himself, garlanded with flowers, is suggestive of the Green Man of the Middle Ages.

Castleton is well worth visiting for its caves, but to witness the Garland Day is to be put in touch with a piece of living history.

Garland Dressing

Charlton-on-Otmoor, Oxfordshire

1 May and 19 September

The garland which stands permanently on the rood-screen in the parish church of Charlton-on-Otmoor, is a large cross decorated with greenery. It is almost human in form, with a narrow waist and bell-shaped skirt, leafy head and arms. Twice a year, on May Day and on the village feast day in September, the garland is taken down from its place on the rood screen and dressed with fresh green leaves of box and yew. The children of the village make a procession to the church, carrying home-made crosses decorated with flowers. After the special garland service, they leave their flowery offerings beneath the freshly dressed garland.

Before the Reformation, it is recalled, there used to be two statues on the rood screen, one of St John and one of Our Lady. The statue of the Virgin used to be taken down and carried over Otmoor to be blessed at the Benedictine Friary at Studley. The statues disappeared during the Reformation, but were replaced by a pair of green, figure-like garlands. Now only one of these survives, though this is still referred to by the villagers as 'May Lady'. Up until 1857 the garlands were taken down annually and formed part of the village festivities, but by 1900 both figure-garlands had disappeared. The garlanded-cross is the sole survivor of an ancient village ceremony which reaches back into the earliest days of the church's history.

Grand Wardmote of the Woodmen of Arden

Meriden, Warwickshire
First week in August

The archery competition that takes place at Meriden during the first week of August, at the Woodmen of Arden's Grand Wardmote, lasts for four days. It is the third of the annual wardmotes when archery competitions take place, the others being in June and July.

The society of the Woodmen of Arden was founded in 1785, though they claim their roots go back much deeper into history. After they established their headquarters in Meriden, which is claimed to be the geographical centre of England, they built their Forest Hall there in 1788. Their number is limited to eighty, and admission is virtually by inheritance, it is said. They wear green frock-coats, a buff waistcoat, white trousers and a green, soft-brimmed shooting hat. Their six-foot yew bows are mostly specially made for them at Meriden and their arrows have their equivalent weight in silver stamped on them as was the medieval practice. Their wardmotes, it is claimed, are descended from the ancient forest court-assemblies, and the competitions keep alive the skills that were once such a vital part of our military heritage.

Greenhill Bower and
Court of Array
Lichfield, Staffordshire
Spring Bank Holiday Monday

The City of Lichfield is proud of its customs, particularly its ceremony on the Spring Bank Holiday. This takes the form of a Bower procession, when the tradespeople of the town, together with bands and local organisations in a general carnival parade, make their way to Greenhill. They are accompanied by the Court of Array, along with the Mayor of Lichfield and civic dignitaries, whose job it is to inspect the City's ancient suits of armour that have been specially designed for the occasion.

The Greenhill Bower and the Court of Array were two separate customs that have come to be celebrated together over the passage of years. In the Middle Ages the city guilds used to meet at Greenhill on Whit Monday, bearing garlands of flowers and the emblems of their trade, thought to be a hangover from an earlier custom connected with midsummer. The second ceremony, the meeting of the Court of Array, dates back originally to 1176 when an Act was passed, reaffirmed by Statute in 1285, that all freemen between the ages of fifteen and sixty were to arm themselves, according to their station, and hold themselves ready for inspection by the Commissioners of Array. When Lichfield received its charter in 1553, the High Constable and bailiffs acquired the right to supervise their own inspection, and this was perpetuated in the Court of Array. Every year, the Court Leet elects two 'Dozeners' from each ward in the City, and these present their formal reports to the High Constable when the Court of Array is convened; the High Constable then reports to the Lord Mayor. The whole court proceeds to join the bower procession to inspect the City's suits of armour where they have been made ready for their inspection at Greenhill.

Grovely Rights Day

Great Wishford, Wiltshire

29 May

The people of Great Wishford rise early on the morning of Oak Apple Day in order to enact an ancient custom that celebrates their right to gather wood from nearby Grovely Wood. Making as much noise as they can to wake their neighbours, they go to the woods. There they gather boughs from oak and other trees, which they bear back to the village, some to decorate their houses. One large branch is specially selected and adorned with ribbons. This is dubbed 'the marriage bough', and is hauled to the top of the church tower to bring luck to couples who are married that year. Then a party of villagers travel to Salisbury Cathedral with four women specially dressed in old-fashioned, rustic clothes and carrying oak-sprays. The four ladies dance up the nave of the cathedral, followed by the accompanying villagers. Then they all stand in front of the altar and cry 'Grovely, Grovely, Grovely! And all Grovely!'

When they return to Great Wishford, there is a procession through the village led by the band. Two men carry the Grovely banner decorated with oak apple motifs, which proclaims: 'Grovely! Grovely! Grovely! And all Grovely! Unity is Strength!' The four ladies walk behind the banner with bundles of wood on their heads, followed by the rest of the village with oak boughs.

There is a Wishford Oak Apple Society lunch, followed by sports and games and general merriment, and a May Queen is crowned.

The Grovely Rights Day goes back to 1603, when a court was held in Grovely Wood to settle a dispute between the village and the local earl concerning grazing and wood-gathering rights. The court heard that:

> '...the olde custome is and time out of mind hath byn that the people and inhabitants of Wishford and Barford aforesaid may lawfully gather and bring away all kinde of deade snappinge wood Boughes and stickes that be in the Woods at Grovely at their pleasure without controlment and none other besides them may lawfully fetch any there at any time.'

To perpetuate the rights, the villagers were:

> '...to goe in a daunce to the Cathedral Church of our blessed ladie in the Cittie of New Sarum ... and theire make theire clayme to theire custome in the Forrest of Grovely in these words: Grovely, Grovely and all Grovely.'

Originally the custom took place on Whit Tuesday, but was transferred, in common with innumerable other local customs, to Oak Apple Day, in a surge of popular enthusiasm for the Restoration. Also, the practice of dancing all the way to Salisbury Cathedral, six miles away, has given way to the comforts of a hired coach, which is quicker, if less picturesque.

Guy Fawkes Carnival

Bridgwater, Somerset

Thursday nearest 5 November

The Bridgwater Guy Fawkes Carnival is now a huge event which has almost lost touch with its origins. It is the first of a circuit of carnivals which take place over the following ten days. However, they do have their own unique firework display in the High Street itself, which is known as 'Bridgwater squibbing'. Over a hundred young people, representatives from numerous carnival clubs, form up in two facing lines. Each has a six-foot pole, attached to the end of which is a squib or roman candle. A row of fire is lit between the two lines, and on a loud blast from the leader's whistle, the two lines of pole-bearers light the touch-papers of their fireworks, which they then raise over their heads. There follows a stupendous, climactic firework display which can be seen for miles.

The carnival itself was first officially organised in 1882 and as it grew in size, so it was moved from Guy Fawkes night to Bridgwater's nearest early-closing day on Thursday. There are now over a hundred separate floats in the carnival, each one competing for the various prizes on offer, which is the reason why Guy Fawkes now plays only a minor role.

Hare Pie Scramble and Bottle-Kicking
Hallaton, Leicestershire
Easter Monday

There is a curious two-part custom that takes place on Easter Monday at the Leicester village of Hallaton. The first part is the scramble for hare pie and the second, and much more robust, is the bottle-kicking. Half the hare pie (though this has traditionally been made of beefsteak) is distributed and eaten outside the church.

The villagers then proceed carrying the 'bottles', which are in fact small wooden barrels bound with iron hoops, to Hare Pie Bank where the remainder of the hair pie is scrambled for by children and others keen enough for the fray. Two of the barrels are full of beer and one of them is empty. The barrels are in turn thrown up three times and on the third drop are seized by the crowd. The bottle-kicking commences, with the native Hallatonians against the rest, chiefly from the neighbouring parish of Medbourne. The goals are variously said to be a stream, a hedge or the parish boundary, and when one has been scored with one barrel, another is brought into play. After the game, the players return to the conical market-cross, which the winners scale and from whence they drink their success from the barrels.

An early description of the origin of the custom is given in the *Annual Register* of 1800, under the heading of 'Antiquities', which shows it goes back some considerable time before then:

'A piece of land was many years ago given, the rents and profits of which the rector for the time being was to receive for his own use, on condition of providing two hare pies, a quantity of ale, and two dozen penny loaves, to be scrambled for on Easter Monday annually, after divine service and a sermon preached.'

Much of the tradition surrounding the events seems to have fallen by the wayside, such as the large procession with a band and a man bearing a pole on the top of which a hare was mounted, but the two customs themselves are very much alive.

Haxey Hood Game

Haxey, Lincolnshire

6 January

The church at Haxey on 6 January (Christmas Day, old-style) is the meeting place for the commencement of one of England's most vigorous and exhausting customs, the Haxey Hood Game. At 2pm, the parties involved march up the village street to the church, singing one of their traditional songs. Foremost among them is the 'Fool'. He is recognisable by his face, which is well-bedaubed with soot and red ochre. Next is the 'Lord of the Hood', with a garlanded top hat and carrying a wand of office, a willow-wand bound according to custom. Then there is the 'Chief Boggin' (Boggan or Boggon), in a red huntsman's coat, and with a garlanded topper bearing the 'Hood', a leather-clad roll about three feet long. He is escorted by the thirteen boggins wearing red football jerseys, or something similar, but always red.

The Fool makes a feeble attempt to get away but the boggins make sure that he takes his stand on the mounting block, or Mowbray Stone, where he makes a speech. This is partly traditional, passed down by word of mouth, and partly extemporary; he also has certain difficulties to surmount, one of which is when damp straw is lit beneath or behind him, enveloping him in clouds of smoke. At the conclusion of his speech, he delivers the exhortation: 'Hoose agin hoose; toon agin toon; if thou meet a man, knock him down – but don't 'urt him!'

Everyone then moves off to a neighbouring field, where the boggins stand guard. Twelve canvas or sacking hoods are then thrown to the ground. Younger players struggle for these and their task is to get hold of one and escape with it to the edge of the field without being intercepted by the boggins.

Once all these twelve hoods have been competed for and carried off, the real business of the day starts. The Hood itself, which has been carried by the Chief Boggin, is thrown down, and what they call the 'sway' begins. The idea is to work the Hood to either one of four pubs at Haxey or the neighbouring village of Westwoodside. Since the Hood cannot be kicked, run off with or thrown, it naturally takes a considerable amount of time and effort before it reaches one of its goals, usually well after dark. The game is over when the landlord of the pub where it finally arrives actually touches the Hood.

It is thought the Haxey Hood Game originated as long ago as the 13th century and was all due to a Lady Mowbray, or de Mowbray, whose family were the local landowners. On Christmas Day, or Epiphany, she was riding from Haxey to Westwoodside, when a sudden gust of wind plucked her red hood from her head and carried it off. Thirteen men, who were employed about the fields, witnessed the mishap and gave chase to the hood, which had to be pursued all over the field before it was seized and presented to her ladyship. Her gratitude was such that she is said to have given the thirteen men, variously: a piece of land; thirteen half-acres of land; or thirteen selions (narrow strips of land). There was a stipulation that, as a commemoration of the event, they must re-enact the chase every year on the same day.

It is for this reason that the boggins wear red, and likewise the Lord of the Hood's wand of office is made up of thirteen willow-wands, bound with thirteen willow-switches. As to the titles, the Fool was the man who caught the hood but was too shy to present it, and the Lord the one who actually made the presentation. At an earlier stage of the proceedings, the Fool was suspended on a rope from a tree and literally 'smoked' over a fire. The Hood itself is an object of reverence, and the predecessor of the current one can be seen in Lincoln Museum. The present one remains in the possession of the landlord of the pub where the last game finished until the following New Year's Eve, when it is collected by the Lord and taken round the neighbouring pubs. It is shown off by the boggins, who sing their handful of songs collecting money for, and interest in, the forthcoming game.

Helston Furry Dance

Helston, Cornwall

8 May (unless this falls on a Sunday or Monday, when it becomes the preceding Saturday)

To see the Helston Furry Dance, it is wise to get there early, as people come from all over the county to enjoy the fun. Basically, it is a day given over entirely to dancing the furry dance to the music of the band playing the well-known but misnamed 'Floral Dance'. There are a number of set dances throughout the day, beginning early in the morning, firstly for young people and then for little children, all of whom are dressed specially for the occasion. The principal dance of the day begins at noon, and sets off from the Guildhall as the clock strikes the hour; participation in this dance is strictly by invitation of the stewards. Some hundreds of morning-coated gentlemen wearing top hats and their elegantly-clad ladies in their long dresses and decorated headgear dance together in an extremely long crocodile right round the town. They dance through the open doors of shops and houses, out into the yards and gardens, then back into the street again, pressed closely by the thousands of sightseers who have thronged into town. The dance takes almost two hours to wend its way down the main street and complete its course.

The shops, houses and pubs have all been decorated with flowers and boughs of greenery, and the obvious closeness of Mayday has led to the confusion over the name, so that in the 18th century it was called the *flora* and in the 19th century the *floral dance*, though it originally stemmed from *feriae*, Latin for festival or holiday, and from which we also derive the word fair. The day of the dance, 8th May, is the feast of the Apparition of St Michael, the patron saint of Helston.

The greenery was originally brought back to the town early in the morning by bands of young people who sang the traditional 'Hal-an-Tow' song, which has come down with innumerable variants, though basically along the lines of the following:

> *Robin Hood and Little John*
> *They both are gone to fair-o*
> *And we will to the merry greenwood*

To see what they do there-o
And for the chase-o, to chase the buck and doe.
Hal an Tow, jolly rumble-o.

And for to fetch the summer home
The summer and the May-o
For summer is a-come-o
And winter is a-gone-o.

Where are the Spaniards
That made so great a boast-o?
For they shall eat the grey goose feathers
And we shall eat the roast-o
In every land, the land where'er we go.

As for St George,
St George he was a knight-o
Of all the knights of Christendom
St George he was the right-o
In every land, the land where'er we go.

God bless Aunt Mary Moses,
With all her power and might-o
And send us peace in merry England
Both by day and night-o,
And send us peace in merry England
Both now and evermore-o.

Hal-an-Tow is variously explained as a variant of heel-and-toe, though native folklorists would have it that it is from the Cornish: *hal* or *hayl* meaning moorland, and *tyow* meaning houses, thus moorland and town – though there seems little reason behind this.

As to St Michael, it is said that the Devil threw a stone at him that missed the saint and landed in the town, and can be seen protruding from the wall of the Angel Inn, which was built around it. The celebration is therefore to welcome the summer and for the deliverance of St Michael.

There is another old inn in Helston, and one that has been continuously brewing its own beer since the 15th century, when it was a monks' rest house. This is the Blue Anchor and visitors should be wary of its strong brew.

Hocktide

Hungerford, Berkshire

Second Tuesday after Easter

The celebration of Hocktide at Hungerford begins at 8 o'clock in the morning on the second Tuesday after Easter, with the blowing of the John O'Gaunt Horn from a window of the Town Hall. This is to summon the commoners to the Hocktide Court, which sits an hour later at 9 o'clock. To make sure the commoners are aware of the summons, the bellman goes out into the streets with cries of 'Oyez!', and a reminder that those who don't attend to answer to their names are liable to a fine.

Meanwhile, two tithing-men, or tutti-men, dressed in top hats and tails, bearing tutti-poles and accompanied by the 'orange-scrambler', begin to make their rounds of the town. In return for watching over the townsmen and their property, the tutti-men are entitled to a fee of a penny from every householder or a kiss from their wives (or husbands) in lieu. This also applies to anyone they meet in the street, commoner or otherwise. If the lady or gentleman of the house doesn't answer the door, the tutti-men are armed with ladders, and exact their fees from the windows. In return for their kisses, an orange is given, taken from a bag by the orange-scrambler and oranges are also presented to any children whom they meet on their rounds.

The survival of the Hocktide festivities at Hungerford is due largely to the rights and privileges granted by John O'Gaunt in 1364. These included fishing rights along the River Kennet, and the grant was confirmed by the gift of the hunting horn. The original of this was replaced in 1634 and bears the inscription: 'John a Gaun did give and grant the Riall of Fishing to Hungerford town from Eldren Stub to Irish Still, excepting som severeal Mill Pound'.

The Hocktide Court has twelve members, called Feoffes, and deals with matters pertaining to the commoners' rights, and the appointment of officers. Hungerford has no mayor but a constable instead, and he presides with his portreeve, bailiff and tithing-men.

There is a traditional Hocktide feast following the official business on the Tuesday and attended by commoners and their guests. After this, there is another custom called 'shoeing the colt'. If a newcomer is spied in their midst, the commoners take hold of the heel of his or her shoe and present the victim to the blacksmith and his assistant for shoeing. A farrier's nail is driven into the heel, until the victim cries out 'Punch!', when he or she is released. For this mercy the victim is supposed to pay for a round of drinks.

Hornblowing

Bainbridge, Yorkshire

27 September to Shrove Tuesday

Every night at 9 o'clock in Bainbridge, in the heart of the ancient forest of Wensleydale, a horn is blown on the village green. It is not known when the custom first started, nor the reason behind it, but by 1823, when first published mention is made of it, it was already looked upon as something from the distant past. It is thought that the horn might have been blown as a guide to lost travellers, and certainly the surrounding area is a desolate place, and must have been more wild and remote in the Middle Ages. Suggestions that the horn-blowing dates back to the Roman occupation seem far-fetched, though there is a Roman fort just outside the village. The horn-blowing duty has been in the hands of the same family for generations, and the present horn is an African buffalo horn, which was presented to the village in 1864. This replaced two previous cows' horns, one dating from 1611, and one of which hangs proudly in the Rose and Crown. There is a rival horn-blowing ceremony at Ripon about thirty miles away.

Hornblowing
Ripon, Yorkshire

Nightly, at 9 o'clock

Every night throughout the year in the City of Ripon, the quaintly-clad Mayor's Hornblower sounds his horn from the four corners of the obelisk in the Market Square. He also sounds a blast outside the mayor's house, to signal that he has discharged his duty.

It is claimed to be the oldest civic custom in Britain and to have begun when Ripon's charter was granted in AD 886 by King Alfred. It is mentioned in 1400, when it was the responsibility of the wakeman, whose office was only replaced by that of mayor in 1604. When the mayor took over the responsibility, along with many others, he appointed his own hornblower, and the job was in single hands right up to 1955, when a deputy was appointed. The incumbent wears a smart fawn coat, with a scarlet collar and cuffs, and a tricorn hat. His horn was specially fashioned in 1865, replacing that of 1690. The previous horns, along with the original, are treasured city possessions and are brought out on 'horn days' (Easter Sunday, Whit Sunday, August Bank Holiday, Christmas Day and Mayor's Sunday). One is suspended from a splendid baldric adorned with the silver medallions depicting the arms and trades of former wakemen and mayors.

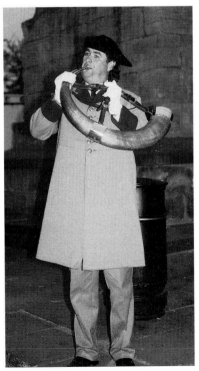

The wakemen had a central role in Ripon's early days, and still emblazoned over the Town Hall is the legend: 'EXCEPT YE LORD KEEP YE CITTIE YE WAKEMAN WAKETH IN VAIN'.

Hunting the Earl of Rone

Combe Martin, Devon

Spring Bank Holiday weekend

The present custom, a resurrection of one buried in the mists of the past, was born again in 1974. This was thanks to a Barnstaple councillor and a group of locals with an interest in folklore and customs, who researched into 'the hunting of the Earl of Rone', an account of which was written up by the Rev G. Tugwell in a book of his travels, *The North Devon Scenery Book* (1863). He had visited the Pack of Cards pub in Combe Martin and talked to three elderly customers who had described the custom, banned by local bye-laws in 1837, because of 'licentiousness and drunken behaviour'.

The Earl of Rone was thought to be a legend about the Earl of Tyrone, Hugh O'Neil, who, following the death of Queen Elizabeth, had been summoned to London, but, warned that he was to be accused of treason, fled first to France and then to Spain. Speculation that he might have been shipwrecked on the North Devon coast is thought to have initiated the legend.

Today's custom begins on the Friday evening at 7.30 pm, when a number of persons, dressed in scarlet soldiers' jackets, bearing mock rifles and wearing conical hats covered in ribbons, march through the village to the sound of drums. These are the 'Grenadiers', and they are accompanied by a circular Hobby Horse who is attended by a Fool carrying a besom. The procession reaches the Top George pub, which is a stable for the Horse.

On Saturday morning, a similar procession takes place, enacted by children from the local primary school, and it too travels round the village. In the evening there is a barn-dance at the town hall, where all are welcome.

On Sunday afternoon, the procession of Friday evening is re-enacted, concluding at the Top George but this time with music provided by accordians, melodians and fiddles.

Bank Holiday Monday sees the final procession, the Grenadiers leaving the Top George and proceeding up the lane to Lady's Wood. They are followed by two ladies leading a donkey. The Grenadiers find the Earl of Rone in the wood and, following a mock-fight, he is captured and brought back mounted back-to-front, on the donkey. Thereafter, there are numerous events wherein the Earl is frequently executed and revived again. All this culminates on the beach when the Grenadiers, carrying the Earl, run to the water's edge and throw him into the sea.

Hurling

St Columb Major, Cornwall

Shrove Tuesday and second Saturday following

Hurling the silver ball at St Columb Major is a boisterous contest and one of the two survivors of this traditional Cornish game (the other takes place at St Ives) that was once common throughout the county. In St Columb, the ball, about the size of a cricket ball and covered in silver, is 'cast up' in the market square by a local dignitary or specially invited guest. The contest then commences between the Townsmen and the Countrymen, the object being to score a goal in one of two ways. The Town goal is a stone trough at Cross Putty, a mile south-west of the square, and the Country goal is a similar trough on the Wadebridge road, a mile to the north. If either of these goals seems unattainable, a goal can be scored by taking the ball outside the parish boundary, though this is further than either of the goals and is now complicated by modern motorways. The winner, that is the one who scores a goal, is carried back in triumph to the market square, where he 'calls up' the ball at 8 o'clock in the evening, if the game has finished by then. The silver ball is then taken round the pubs to the strains of the hurling song:

> *For we roll, we roll the Town ball along*
> *And we roll, we roll the Town ball along*
> *And we roll, we roll the Town ball along*
> *And we all come marching home.*

(Though it might be the 'Country' ball, depending on the winner.)

The ball is dipped into jugs of beer, thus bestowing on them the accolade of 'silver beer' and these are then consumed by all. The scorer can keep the ball until the following year, and it is used until a new one has been donated. It bears the inscription:

> *Town and country do your best*
> *For in this parish I must rest.*

The hurling at St Columb is extremely well documented and has even become the subject of a book in its own right, *The Silver Ball* by Ivan

Raby. An early description of the game is given by Richard Carew in his *Survey of Cornwall* in 1602:

'The ball in this game may be compared to an infernal spirit; for whosoever catcheth it fareth straightaways like a mad man, struggling and fighting those that go about to hold him; and no sooner is the ball gone from him, but he respiteth the fury to the next receiver and himself becometh peaceable as before.'

In 1654 a demonstration of the game was given by a hundred Cornishmen in Hyde Park before 'His Highness the Lord Protector and many of the Privy Council and divers eminent gentlemen'. And in 1725, Daniel Defoe, in his *Tour Through the Whole Island of Great Britain,* wrote:

'The game called Hurlers, is a thing the Cornishmen value themselves much upon; I must confess, I see nothing in it, but that it is a rude violent play among the boors, or country people; brutish and furious, and a sort of evidence, that they were once a kind of barbarian.'

Let us leave the last word to the natives. An early inscription on the silver ball reads, in Cornish, *Guare wheag yn guare teag*, or fair play is good play.

Hurling the Silver Ball

St Ives, Cornwall

First Monday after Candlemas (2nd February)

It is the children of St Ives who compete for the silver ball on their patron saint's day, and the mayor who starts the game by throwing the ball into play. This takes place about 10.30 in the morning, after the ball has been traditionally blessed at the saint's holy well. The ball, made of wood and covered with silver, about the size of a tennis ball, is fought for on the beach at a place depending on the tide. The winner is the one who has it in his possession at noon, and he is entitled to a small cash prize on returning the ball to the mayor.

This is a genteel survival of a hurling contest that was once general throughout Cornwall, a much rougher adult version taking place to this day at St Columb Major on Shrove Tuesday. St Ia, the patron saint of St Ives, is said to have floated over from Ireland on a leaf, and it would seem that the reason the hurling takes place on her feast day is a contribution to the celebration of her name.

John Knill's Charity

St Ives, Cornwall

25 July, every five years (2001, 2006 etc)

Every fifth year on St James' Day, at Knill's Steeple on Worvas Hill overlooking St Ives, there is enacted a picturesque ceremony that commemorates the name of John Knill. The Mayor of St Ives and other civic dignitaries, all wearing white rosettes, proceed up a steep hill to Knill's Monument. They are accompanied by ten girls under the age of ten dressed in white, two elderly widows and a fiddler. On arrival at the monument the ten small girls dance round the steeple for fifteen minutes to the music of the fiddle. When they have finished dancing they all sing the 'Old Hundredth' psalm. The proceedings are supervised by the two widows and on completion of this brief ceremony, the girls, widows and fiddler all receive a modest sum of money for their pains.

The ceremony was conceived by John Knill to perpetuate his memory, and it has succeeded in doing so ever since he died in 1811, and even before then. He built his steeple out of granite in 1782, when he was customs officer in the area. He had been Mayor of St Ives in 1767, planned the terms of his bequest in 1797, and had the ceremony acted out in 1801. The steeple was to be his mausoleum but he was thwarted in this part of his design by his death and subsequent burial in London, due to some complications over the consecration.

Other beneficiaries of John Knill's bequest were to be a married couple over the age of 60 with the largest family, who had not sought relief from the parish; the finest net-maker; the best pilchard-packer; two of the best 'follow boys', or fishing apprentices; and a recently married girl who was thought to be most worthy. There were other beneficiaries, in the tinning as well as the fishing industry, and finally, there was to be a dinner for the trustees. All this to come out of the £100 every five years. The bequest is carried out today as best as can be, allowing for the decline in the value of money. This has been more matched by the decline in the tinning and fishing industry in the area, which is now a modest artist's colony, more reliant on tourism.

Kiplingcotes Derby

South Dalton, Yorkshire

Third Thursday in March

Adherents of the Kiplingcotes Derby claim it is the oldest flat race in the world. It takes place on the third Thursday in March at South Dalton, and begins sometime around noon, when all the official proceedings have been concluded. It is run from South Dalton to the finish, near Kiplingcotes Farm, a distance of about four miles, some of it over roads, some over paths. The winner gets the interest on the trust and the runner-up collects the stake money, which all entrants have to pay, and which is often more than that claimed by the winner.

It all began in 1519, and it was thought to have been held off and on for the next hundred years. It was in 1618 that the Earl of Burlington, together with various peers, knights and gentlemen, subscribed a sum of money to endow the race 'in perpetuity'. Under the 'Articles to be Observed and Kept', it is stated that the entrants have each to put up £4; that the horses shall be led out between 12 and 1 o'clock, and that the race shall be run before 2 o'clock; that the rider shall weigh ten stone; that every rider shall put his stake into the clerk's hand on or before 11 o'clock; that horses that are pulled back shall win no prize; and that any rider who interferes with another shall win no prize. There are fourteen such articles in all, and they are read out to the riders before the start of the race, and after they have handed over their stake money and have been weighed.

The 'Kibling Coates' race dates back to long before the Derby was first run in 1780. It takes place no matter what the weather or conditions: indeed, on one occasion a carthorse was led round on its own when there were no other entrants.

Knights of the Old Green Competition
Southampton, Hampshire
First Wednesday in August and following days

The tournament for a Knighthood of the Old Green, Lower Canal Walk takes place in Southampton on what is claimed to be the oldest bowling green in the country. It commences at 3 o'clock in the afternoon, graced by the presence of the mayor, on the first Wednesday in August. The contestants are Gentlemen Commoners and the officials are Knights of the Green, those who have earned their knighthoods previously. The commoners wear whites and club-ties, and the knights are dressed in morning suits and top hats. The first man to win seven 'ends' is acclaimed a Knight of the Green. It is a process that can take a number of days, as there may be any number of players and each bowls two woods. The distance from the wood to the jack is carefully measured and recorded, the woods being removed for the next contestant. At a splendid ceremony later, the Knight is installed and hereafter addressed with his new title of Sir, his wife earning the title of Lady. By all accounts, it is an expensive honour, both sartorially and in terms of drinks dispensed to fellow knights.

It is said there has been a lawn on the Old Green since 1187, though it was not recorded as a bowling green until 1299. The Southampton Old Bowling Green Club was formed in 1705 and the tournament initiated by a man named Miller on 1 August 1776. Bowls were played here for a time in the 16th century when it was unlawful for commoners to play the game, archery being thought a more patriotic pastime, and in 1894 the Council investigated the Club's rights to the Green. It was found that 'although the ground itself no doubt belongs to the town, the present club who occupy and manage the Green would appear to have obtained prescriptive rights through length of usure'. Squatters' rights, no less.

Lewes Bonfire Night

Lewes, Sussex

5 November

Guy Fawkes Night is celebrated at Lewes in Sussex with an enthusiasm that must make it the most spectacular of all bonfire nights. Throughout the evening, the numerous bonfire societies foregather at the War Memorial, where they lay wreaths, and on occasion sing hymns. Thereafter, there is the Grand Parade, with flaming torches and members of each society dressed up in striking costumes according to their chosen theme, such as Vikings, Zulus or Red Indians. Each society marches to its own bonfire site, where 'prelates' or 'archbishops' read a sermon before exploding effigies of the Pope and Guy Fawkes.

It is not forgotten in Lewes that seventeen Protestant martyrs were burned to death here in the reign of Queen Mary, and one of the societies to this day still carries 'No Popery' banners. In 1679 a Benjamin Harris described the burning of a popish effigy, and in 1853 the first two bonfire societies were formed, the Borough and the Cliffe Society, and many more have been formed since.

Parliament instituted 5 November as 'a holiday forever in thanksgiving to God for deliverance and detestation of the papistry, to commemorate Guy Fawkes' failed plot of 1605 to blow up the Houses of Parliament'. The people of Lewes are not likely to let the occasion pass unremarked.

Lot-meadow Drawing

Yarnton, Oxfordshire

Week following 29 June

The Yarnton Lot-meadow Drawing ceremony is now the surest remembrance of a custom which was of the utmost importance to the tenants of the surrounding countryside. The day after the auction of the lots in the meadow, which takes place in the Grapes Inn, the 'meadsman' summons the tenants to a corner of the meadow itself for the disposal of the lots. Each lot of the meadow has a name, endowed by a tenant in the past. These are variously: Gilbert, White, Harry, Boat, William of Bladon, Parry, Walter Geoffrey, Watery Molly, Freeman Green, Bolton, Dunne and Rothe; there is another, belonging to the church in perpetuity, called the Tidals. The meadsman has a bag containing thirteen cherry-wood balls, known as the mead balls, and each one bears the name of one of the lots. These are drawn individually from the bag, and the current possessor of the named lot is given the first strip in the meadow, the others following as their names appear.

Thus each tenant had a different strip each year, ensuring that they all had an equal chance of acquiring a richer or poorer part of the meadow, as the case might be. After the draw, each lot was carefully paced out, marked with a stake, and the new tenant's initials cut in the turf after being exposed with a cut of the scythe. The hay was mown shortly afterwards, each strip being easily identifiable by its owner.

The lot-drawing and distribution of the plots was a practice that hails from Anglo-Saxon times in the 6th and 7th centuries. Machinery has done away today with the common effort of mowing that used to take place, when the whole pasture of some eighty-one acres had to be mowed in a day, and men came from the surrounding countryside to help with the mowing. At one time, the lot-meadow mowing was the occasion of a feast, or unofficial fair, with a race for a garland at the end of the day and much merry-making. The festivities were dampened somewhat after 1817, when there was much disorder and a man was killed. It was this, and the use of agricultural machinery, that has made the custom now little more than a pleasant old-fashioned ritual.

Marbles Championship
Tinsley Green, near Crawley, Sussex
Good Friday

It is claimed that marbles has been played at Tinsley Green for hundreds of years, though the current championship games, which take place on Good Friday, hark back to its revival in 1932. The game is basically quite simple. There is a sand-covered cement ring, six feet across, on which there are placed forty-nine marbles. The object is to knock as many of these out of the ring as you can by projecting your shooting-marble, or tolley, into their midst. The tolley is placed in the crook of your first finger and fired by the thumb, without moving the hand, which is held outside the ring. Teams compete in turn, and the highest scorers from each then play individually for the British Marbles Championship.

Some say that competitive marbles goes back to 1600, and certainly *Notes and Queries* in 1879 says that: 'From time immemorial, marbles playing has been popular in Sussex; in some parts of the county Ash Wednesday, as well as Good Friday, has been known as "Marbles Day".' And in 1934 the *Daily Mail* reported the third annual marble match between Surrey and Sussex, saying that in the old days, 'marbles was the favourite sport in Sussex'.

Marshfield Paper Boys

Marshfield, Gloucestershire

Boxing Day

The Marshfield mummers, known as the Paper Boys, perform their play in the village street a number of times on Boxing Day morning, starting at about 11 o'clock. They wear costumes that are covered with strips of paper, giving them a truly tatterdemalion appearance, and they carry wooden swords. They are led by one of their number, known as the Town Crier, who opens the performance with 'Oyez, Oyez, Oyez!'

It is not known for how long the Marshfield mummers have performed their traditional play here. What is known is that it had all been forgotten by 1930, when the vicar of the day overheard his gardener reciting some part of the play. He told his sister, Violet Alford, an eminent folklorist, who immediately set about resurrecting the mummers, and saw to the play's first revival on Boxing Day in 1931. The Town Crier apart, there are eight characters, and the performance is concluded with a song. The Marshfield Paper Boys have rewarded the faith of their revivalist and enlivened many a Boxing Day since.

May Morning

Magdalen College, Oxford

1 May

At 6 o'clock on the morning of May Day, the choristers of Magdalen College sing a Latin hymn from the top of their tower. The singing is followed by a peal of bells, and is the signal for the morris dancers below in the High Street to begin their lively and colourful welcome to the first day of May. Large crowds traditionally gather at this hour in the High Street and on Magdalen Bridge to listen to the hymn and to watch the morris dancers, who dance during the next few hours at various appointed places in the City, around the Radcliffe Camera, St Giles and Broad Street.

There are various theories regarding the origins of the popular May Day custom. One is that Lord Berkeley, who died in 1491, made a generous bequest to Magdalen, and that it is an annual requiem in his memory. Another is that it was as a memorial service for Henry VII, who died in 1509. More likely is that it was a celebration of the completion of the tower on the same date. Halfway through the 17th century it had virtually become a concert. 'The choral ministers of this house', it was declared at that time, 'do according to ancient custom salute Flora every year on the first of May at 4 o'clock in the morning with vocal music of several parts; which, having been performed, hath given great content to the neighbourhood and the auditors underneath.'

The briefer and less generous performance today, at a more congenial hour, is thought to have come about through a drenching the choristers received in the 18th century, when they only had time to sing part of their college grace before seeking shelter.

Mayor of Ock Street
Abingdon, Oxfordshire

Saturday nearest 19 June

A survival from an ancient feast-day celebration at Abingdon in Oxfordshire is the election of the 'mock mayor', known as the Mayor of Ock Street. A ballot-box is placed in the street outside a pub, and all residents of Ock Street are entitled to a vote, as are all members of the traditional Abingdon Morris Dancers. The custom begins with morris dancing in the morning, and at 4.30 in the afternoon the name of the new mayor is announced. He is presented with his regalia, a top hat, a sash of office, a sword and a mazer, or silver-inlaid hardwood drinking bowl, said to be over 200 years old. He receives the Ock Street Horns, ox horns mounted on a wooden pole. He is then carried round all the pubs in Ock Street by the morris dancers, seated in a wooden chair decorated with flowers; this is borne on two long poles and preceded by the horn-bearer.

Morris dancing in Abingdon is documented in the churchwardens' records of 1560, where an entry concerns 'two dossin Morres Belles, 1s.' The custom of electing mock mayors was also common elsewhere in England – though there are few survivals today. Abingdon feast day commemorated the Translation of St Edmund of Abingdon, and it is said that in 1700 an ox was roasted in the street, meat from which was distributed to the poor. A fight developed afterwards between uptown and downtown for the possession of the ox horns, and the leader of the winning side was a morris dancer by the name of Hemmings. He was also the squire of the morris dancers, who have kept possession of the horns ever since.

Maypole Raising

Barwick-in-Elmet, Yorkshire

Spring Bank Holiday Tuesday,
every three years (1999, 2002 etc)

Every third year on Easter Monday in the village of Barwick-in-Elmet near Leeds, the village maypole, almost ninety feet high and surmounted by a fox weather-vane, is taken down from its position and carried by the men to a local field for repainting and decorating. Three Pole Men are elected by the villagers to supervise the job and to oversee the re-erection on Spring Bank Holiday Tuesday. When it is ready to be put in place, four specially prepared garlands are fixed halfway up the pole, and these are hung with bells attached to red-white-and-blue ribbons. The event takes place early in the evening and requires the combined might of nearly 200 men, along with ropes, ladders and pulleys. It is a day of general celebration, with a procession, sports and music, and the crowning of the May Queen.

Some say the custom dates from 'time immemorial'; others have it that it has been observed since 'before the advent of Christianity'. The pole is traditionally made of two spliced larch poles and has been renewed over the years.

Midsummer Day Ritual
Stonehenge, near Amesbury, Wiltshire
21 June

Latter-day Druids conduct a dawn service at Stonehenge on Midsummer's Day. The sun rises exactly in line with the altar and hele stones, and the Druids foregather in the darkness to be there so they can observe the sun precisely as it rises on the horizon. Many others have been congregating at Stonehenge in recent years, so much so that there is now a large police presence to prevent any damage to Britain's most famous prehistoric monument.

Stonehenge, about which books are constantly being written, was built as a sun temple about 2600 BC, and it is thought that it was continuously used as a place of worship up to about 1400 BC. The present Druid revival began in 1740 after the publication of William Stukeley's *Stonehenge, a Temple Restor'd to the British Druids*.

Minehead Hobby Horse

Minehead, Somerset

30 April to 3 May

The Minehead Hobby Horse emerges on the eve of May Day, or 'warning eve', from his home on the quay. He visits the local pubs, chases the children and cavorts in the streets while his attendants collect money. He is followed by musicians, with drums and melodeons. This is the Sailor's Horse, and he is occasionally challenged by another, impertinent Town Horse.

The Sailor's Horse is up by 6 o'clock on the next morning, when he trots up Higher Town to Whitecross, where he bows three times to the rising sun. His other formal engagement on May Day is to pay a visit to Dunster Castle, where he himself is entertained and where he entertains in return. On 2 May and 3 May, he visits various outlying hamlets, returning eventually to finish his dancing in Minehead on the evening of 3 May.

As with the Padstow Horse, there is nothing certain about the origins of the Minehead Horse. There is a suggestion from both Padstow and Minehead that their own is the original and the other the imitation horse. The Minehead horse is credited with frightening off Viking invaders in AD 878 and 1052. Though if this is to be believed, it scotches the theory that it is a commemoration of a famous shipwreck near Dunster in 1772, when a cow was washed ashore, whose tail was cut off and became part of the horse. In a report of 1830, the custom is said then to have 'prevailed for ages'. And as to the horse's peregrinations, it is claimed that these make it part of a beating-the-bounds custom.

The creature itself is long and boat-shaped, borne in the middle from whence the head emerges. This wears a mask fashioned out of tin and crowned with ribbons and feathers, like the helmet of an armoured knight. The horse's upper part is covered with ribbons which flow in the wind, and the sides are decorated with circles. At the rear is a long, tasselated tail. Musicians apart, the Town Horse is attended by 'Gullivers' (derivation uncertain), wearing masks and tall hats, with ribbon covered costumes. Their job is to collect money, which they do with enthusiasm, but not quite with such vigour as they did in the past, when it is said they actually went so far as to kill a man who was reluctant to offer a donation.

Olney Pancake Race

Olney, Buckinghamshire

Shrove Tuesday

Tradition has it that the race was first run in 1445, pancakes being a popular dish and receiving royal favour. It was run on Shrove Tuesday, the day before Lent, and was followed by a festival of celebration, pranks and pastimes. The race has continued down the centuries, while many other local customs died out. The race itself lapsed occasionally, though it was never entirely forgotten by the womenfolk of Olney.

After the last major lapse, during the Second World War, it was revived again in 1948 by the then vicar, the Rev Canon Ronald Collins, when he came across some old photographs dating from the 1920s and 30s, showing the local women running along with frying pans. Hoping to revive the ancient custom, he called for volunteers, and thirteen women presented themselves on Shrove Tuesday that year. The race immediately caught the popular imagination and has flourished ever since. Today the race is run from the Market Place to a point midway down Church Lane, some 415 yards. Warning bells are rung from the church and the race is started by the churchwarden at 11.55 am, using the bronze Pancake Bell on display at the museum. Pancakes are tossed at the start and have to be tossed again by the winner. After the race the runners, officials, townsfolk and visitors enter the church for the Shriving Service, when traditional Olney hymns are sung. The frying pans are placed round the font and the runners occupy their reserved seats. Following the service the official prizes are presented.

Competitors must be women of eighteen years or older and have lived in Olney for at least three months prior to the event or, if temporarily away, have a permanent residence in the town.

In 1950 the race became an international event, a challenge having been received from the town of Liberal, in Kansas USA, where they had seen press photographs of the race, and decided to start a similar custom. The international challenge has continued ever since.

Oranges and Lemons Service
St Clement Danes, Strand, London WC2
Weekday near 31 March

On or near 31 March every year, at St Clement Danes in the Strand, the Oranges and Lemons Service takes place. This is a children's service, attended by the pupils of St Clement Danes primary school. They read the lesson, recite the famous nursery rhyme and, on occasions, play the tune on handbells. At the conclusion of the service, each one is presented with an orange and a lemon from a table outside the church (if dry). The nursery rhyme, which begins with the lines:

> *Oranges and lemons*
> *Say the bells of St Clement's*

was first recorded in *Tommy Thumb's Poetry Song Book* in about 1744, sung to the tune familiar to every child in the country. When the bells were restored to St Clement Danes in 1920, after they had been silent since 1913 when their timbers were found to be dangerous, the vicar decided to inaugurate the service for children. On 31 March that year, he distributed the oranges and lemons for the first time, which he persuaded the Danish community in London to donate. This continued until 1940 when, during the Second World War, the church was nearly destroyed by bombing. In 1957 the church was restored as a memorial to the RAF, and the familiar carillon now rings out at 9 o'clock, at noon and at 6 o'clock in the evening.

The Danish association is unclear, though it is said that Harold Harefoot, son of King Canute, was buried here in 1040, and there was at some stage a massacre of Vikings in the vicinity.

Padstow Hobby Horse

Padstow, Cornwall

1 May

May Day is celebrated in Padstow with an enthusiasm that is not matched anywhere else in the country. After the stroke of midnight, and a foregathering around the Maypole in the square, the people outside the Golden Lion Inn begin to sing the so-called 'Night-song', greeting the landlord and his wife:

> *Rise up, Mr Hawken, and joy to you betide,*
> *For summer is acome unto today*
> *And bright is your bride that lies beside your side,*
> *In the merry month of May.*

Having roused Mr Hawken (or whoever the landlord might currently be) from his bed – if he'd managed to get to bed at all with the impending excitement – the crowd of 'Mayers' moves off to serenade other neighbours, fitting in the name to suit the verses. For a young girl, it is:

> *Rise up, Miss —, all in your smock of silk*
> *And all your body under as white as any milk!*

And for a man of means:

> *Rise up, Mr —, I know you well afine*
> *You have a shilling in your purse*
> *and I wish it were mine!*

The singing goes on until the victim appears at the window to greet the singers. The Mayers continue with their singing until about 2 o'clock in the morning, when they disperse to preserve their energies for May Day proper, and the coming of the Obby Oss, or osses, since there are now a number of the creatures.

The first one (though a recent rival), the Blue Ribbon Oss, also known as the Temperance or Peace Oss, bursts forth from the Institute steps at 10 o'clock in the morning, to the accompaniment of the music of the band and the drumming that will continue throughout the day. It is a large, black, circular creature about six feet wide, like an enormous hooped skirt, with a small decorated horse head protruding from one side and a short tail from the other. The bearer's head emerges from the centre, wearing a conical hat and a grotesque mask.

However, the Temperance Oss is nothing to the 'Old Oss' which makes its triumphant entry from the Golden Lion Inn an hour later at 11 o'clock, accompanied by retainers and followers as was the Temperance Oss, though wearing red as opposed to blue. Each oss has a master of ceremonies and a 'teaser' with a padded leather club.

The Blue Ribbon Oss then begins his tour through the town followed an hour later by the Old Oss.

Accompanied by his band and drummers, the followers sing:

> *Unite and unite and let us all unite*
> *For summer is acome unto today*
> *And whither we are going we will all unite,*
> *In the merry morning of May.*
> *Where are the young men that here and now should dance?*
> *Some they are in England, and some they are in France.*
> *In the merry morning of May*
> *Where are the maidens that here now should sing?*
> *In the merry morning of May*
> *They are in the meadows the flowers gathering.*

To the cries of 'Oss, Oss, wee Oss!', the Oss snatches a pretty girl from the crowd and envelops her in his skirts, which is one of his customary roles and one that naturally delights his followers.

The mood of the music will suddenly fall, taking on a dirge-like air, and the Oss sinks to the ground, as if in a dying swoon, while the followers begin to sing:

> *O Where is St George, O where is he-o?*
> *He's out in his long boat, all on the salt sea-o.*
> *Up flies the kite, down falls the lark-o,*
> *Aunt Ursula Birdwood she had an old ewe*
> *And she died in her park-o.*

The teaser caresses the Oss with his club and the crowd all take pity on him, until suddenly the drums start to beat furiously again, the Oss leaps up to his feet and the followers sing another refrain of the May Song.

With the merry ring, adieu the merry Spring,
For summer is acome unto today,
How happy is the little bird that merrily does sing
In the merry morning of May.

The Oss continues his dancing through the streets of the town throughout the day, until he comes to meet the rival Oss at the maypole in Broad Street, sometime during the evening. They are both then allowed to rest from their exertions until the next year.

As with many old customs, the origins of the Padstow Obby Oss are shrouded in the past. The hobby horse is not unique to Padstow, there being a rival one at Minehead in Somerset – and at festivals elsewhere, though not necessarily on May Day. There is a reference to the Padstow version in a history of Cornwall in 1803 and a description of it 'being extended with hoops and painted to resemble a horse' in 1824; there is even a sketch of the horse's mask from 1835. The present mask worn by the bearer is thought to have been brought back in 1860 by a sailor, from Africa or the South Seas. The Oss is no longer accompanied by twelve little girls dressed in white, as once it was; neither does it make its visit to Treator Pool outside the town, where it took a drink and splashed the onlookers, nor to the sea at the slipway.

The introduction of the Blue Ribbon Oss began at the turn of the century, when it was felt that the original Oss's celebrations were turning into bacchanalia. The Temperance Oss appeared intermittently until 1919, when it was reincarnated as a 'Peace Oss', and money was collected by his followers for charity, as it still is along with the 'Old Oss' collection. Though the followers of each Oss are fanatical in their devotion, there is no longer the outright antagonism that there once was.

It has been a long-held belief that any young girl who has been ensnared by the Oss will be brought good luck, and gain a husband or bear a child over the next twelve months – though not necessarily both, or in that order.

One version of the origins of the Obby Oss has it that it dates back to the 6th century, when St Petroc came over from Wales to found the monastery at Petroskowe (Padstow). The saint captured a fearsome local dragon, which he led out to sea. The teaser is seen as the saint and the Oss as the dragon, explaining the no-longer honoured diversion to the slipway. Led by 'Aunt Ursula Birdwood' and followed by the women of Padstow, the Oss is also said to have helped frighten off the marauding French, while the young men were either in England or France, as the song had it.

Whatever else, the Padstow Obby Oss is very much alive today and takes to his annual May Day outing with as much enthusiasm as he did two hundred years ago.

Penny Hedge
Whitby, Yorkshire

Ascension Eve

There is a strange gathering on the foreshore near Boyes Staithe in Whitby Harbour at 9 o'clock on the morning of Ascension Eve. A tenant of the Manor of Whitby, overseen by the manor's bailiff, constructs a hedge (or fence), in the sand. A number of staves are driven into the mud and these are woven together with osiers, pliant strips of willow, or some other wood. The finished hedge is about five feet high and ten feet long and on completion the bailiff blows his horn and cries out: 'Out on ye! Out on ye!' The Penny Hedge, or horngarth, is planted below the high-tide mark and has to be strong enough to withstand three tides. The ceremony is watched by curious onlookers from the roadway above.

Though some say the custom began in Saxon times, the legend has it that it began in 1159, during the reign of Henry II, and came about as follows. Three young gentlemen were hunting a boar in the woods of the abbey at Eskdaleside when the boar fled into a chapel occupied by a hermit, or monk at prayer, from the abbey. He barred entrance to the pursuing hounds, and the hunters were so enraged at his interference that they savagely beat him. As he lay dying, he asked the abbot to forgive them for what was about to become a murder, provided they carried out a penance for 'the safeguard of their souls'. They and their descendants, who were tenants of the abbey, were only to keep their lands if they performed the following service annually on Ascension Eve. The stipulations were that they:

> 'Shall come to the Wood of the Trayhead ... and there shall the Officer of the Abbot blow his horn, to the intent that you may know how to find him, and he shall deliver unto you, William de Bruce, ten stakes, ten Stout-Stowers and ten Yedders, to be cut by you... with a knife of a Penny Price; and you Ralphe de Piercie, shall take one and twenty of each sort, to be cut in the same manner; and you Allston, shall take nine of each sort, to be cut as aforesaid; and to be taken on your backs, and carried to the town of Whitby and so to be there before nine of the Clock

(if it be full Sea, to cease service), as long as it is low water, at nine of the Clock, the same hour each of you shall set your Stakes at the Brim of the Water, each stake a yard from another, and so Yedder them, as with Yedders, and so Stake on each side with your Stout-Stowers that they stand three Tides without removing by the Force of the Water... And if you and your successors do refuse this Service, so long as it not be full sea at that Hour aforesaid, you and yours shall forfeit all your lands to the Abbot, or his successors.'

The terms of the penance are carried out to this day, though the abbey is in ruins, and those who observe it are not directly related to the perpetrators of the murder. The Manor of Whitby has taken over the land and oversees the custom. As to the Penny Hedge, it is not known whether this is a corruption of penance, or refers to the penny knife. A horngarth is an enclosure for cattle, and leads some to believe the ceremony predates the events of 1159. The cry 'Out on ye!' is thought to be an expression of disapproval, such as 'shame on you!'.

Pretty Maid's Charity

Holsworthy, Devon

Second Wednesday in July

St Peter's Fair in Holsworthy is proclaimed by the Town Crier at 8 o'clock on the second Wednesday morning in July, but the exciting event of the day is the arrival of the hitherto unknown winner of the Pretty Maid's Charity. She emerges from the church door as the clock strikes noon and she is escorted across the road on the arm of the Portreeve to pay an official visit to the fair.

This pleasant charity dates back only to 1841, and was the bequest of the Rev Thomas Meyrick, a brother of the rector of Holsworthy, who left a small sum of money – £2 10s invested in government stock – the interest to be paid annually 'to the young single woman resident of Holsworthy under 30 years of age who is generally esteemed by the young as the most deserving, the most handsome, and the most noted for her quietness and attendance at church'. He hoped that this well-meant example might 'lead rulers to see and know that subjects are better directed and led by harmless amusement and by judicious rewards than by fear and punishment'.

The Pretty Maid is selected by the trustees, and her identity is kept secret until the moment she emerges from the church, which means she has been kept hiding in the vestry since early that morning. After visiting the fair with the Portreeve, she is entertained at an official lunch, and is called upon later in the year for other occasional duties.

Purbeck Marblers and Stonecutters Day
Corfe Castle, Dorset
Shrove Tuesday

The Ancient Order of Purbeck Marblers and Stonecutters holds its annual meeting on Shrove Tuesday at the Town Hall in Corfe Castle. The meeting is a private affair which begins at noon, when the company is summoned by the church bell. Apprentices to be admitted wait in the Fox Inn while the meeting is in session. When they are called to present themselves to the Warden, each one must bring a penny loaf, a quart of ale and 6s 8d. A shilling is levied from each member who has married in the preceding year, save the latest to wed, who must provide a football.

The ceremony becomes public when the football is produced and used for a Shrovetide football game in the streets of Corfe Castle.

The Articles of Association were drawn up in 1651, when the title of 'Ancient' was given to the order, suggesting a history going back well before then. Purbeck marble was much in demand for decorating churches and important buildings, and the Purbeck quarries shipped this, and other stone, from Poole Harbour to masons' workshops in London and other places. There were over 150 members of the order in 1651 – but only a third of that number today. Apprentices in earlier days had to negotiate their bread and beer through a crowd of mocking marblers without spilling any.

The ritual football game once took the players all the way down to Owre Quay in Poole, three miles away, as a custom to keep the roads open for transporting their stone. The road passes through Owre Farm, and by way of payment for the right of passage the order paid a pound of peppercorn, which peppercorn rent is honoured to this day.

Royal Maundy

A different cathedral annually

Maundy Thursday

On Maundy Thursday the Queen herself dispenses the Maundy Money to the poor, at a different venue each year, usually a cathedral. The ceremony commences with two processions: firstly, the Queen's, with the local clergy and her own choir from the Royal Chapel; secondly, the Almonry's, escorted by the Yeomen of the Guard, two of whom bear the purses for the distribution on great silver dishes. After prayers and a reading from the Gospel of St John, the Queen presents the recipients with a small sum of currency of the day in a leather purse, green for women and white for men. There follows a lesson, and the Queen makes the second distribution of red and white purses. The red purse again contains ordinary currency, in lieu of clothes and food, the white with the specially minted Maundy Money. Maundy Money is also presented to the four Children of the Almonry, especially selected locally from the deserving poor.

The Maundy service is one of the few customs that has devolved on the monarch directly from the teachings of Christ; it is performed in many Catholic and Orthodox churches on the Continent. Christ's example was washing the feet of His disciples at the Last Supper, and this was traditionally done by English monarchs, as we know from the example of King John in the 13th century. From the end of the 17th century, the monarch left the duty of dispensing the Maundy Money to the Lord High Almoner until George V personally took it up again in 1932.

The recipients are made up of an equal number of men and women pensioners, one each for every year of the Queen's age and a pair over for grace. The Maundy Money is in sets of ten pence, containing one four-, one three-, one two- and a one-penny piece, a set for each decade of the monarch's age, the balance being made up of single coins. Until recently, the ceremony took place at Westminster Abbey, but by holding it in different parts of the country, a wider distribution of the royal bounty is assured.

St Bartholomew's Bun Race
St Bartholomew's Hospital, Sandwich, Kent
24 August

The Bartlemas Bun Race for children takes place around the chapel of St Bartholomew's Hospital at Sandwich on St Bartholomew's Day, after various traditional ceremonies have preceded it. Each participant receives a currant bun, while the attendant grown-ups are each given a St Bart's Biscuit, impressed with a copy of the hospital's ancient seal.

St Bartholomew's Hospital is an almshouse for sixteen elderly 'brothers and sisters', and was founded on the spoils, it is said, of a great sea battle on St Bartholomew's Day in 1217, when the ships of the Cinque Ports defeated an invading French fleet. The Mayor of Sandwich attends a memorial service to the hospital's founders on that day and witnesses the selection of the new Master for the coming year, after which the race commences. The current custom is thought to replace an earlier one, when a St Bartholomew's Dole of bread, cheese and ale was given out, which could at an earlier time have been enjoyed by pilgrims on their way to Canterbury.

St Wilfrid's Feast Procession

Ripon, Yorkshire

Saturday before first Monday in August

Ripon's annual fair is opened with a pageant round the city led appropriately by a man dressed up as St Wilfrid, and mounted on a white horse. He is an imposing figure with a large beard, bishop's robes and mitre, and carrying a crozier. The pageant contains an impressive array of floats depicting scenes from the city's history, and on the completion of his tour St Wilfrid is welcomed at the west door of the cathedral by the Dean, whereupon a short service of thanksgiving is held.

The fair has been held annually since 1108, when a royal charter was granted. It was originally on St Wilfrid's Feast Day in April, but later transferred to the present date to coincide with Wilfrid's return from exile in AD 686. He founded the minster of Ripon, and in the Middle Ages his effigy used to be borne round the streets at the opening of the fair. This practice was abandoned at the outset of the Reformation, but later continued, as now, with a living representative of the saint. St Wilfrid, who was educated at Lindisfarne, is considered to be one of the most important men of the Old English church.

Sheriff's Ride
Lichfield, Staffordshire

A Saturday near 8 September

Once a year since 1553, on or about the Feast of the Nativity of the Blessed Virgin, the Sheriff of Lichfield has ridden out on horseback to make a tour of the city's boundaries. He sets out shortly after 11 o'clock, after providing some hospitality, and is accompanied by a cavalcade of citizens and civic dignitaries. Calculations as to how many miles are covered vary, but certainly there are a good few, and a number of stops for refreshment are made before the Sheriff is met on his return by the city's Sword and Mace-bearers, and ceremoniously escorted back to the Guildhall.

A charter was granted to the city in 1553, under Queen Mary, which stipulated that a sheriff must be elected, and one of his tasks was to make a tour of the city's boundary. This was confirmed by another charter in 1664, under Charles II. One of the reasons the custom has been kept up so assiduously is that the sheriff elected must accept office, or be liable to a fine, imprisonment and a loss of civic privilege. One of the duties of that office is still the sheriff's ride.

Swan Upping
River Thames, from Sunbury to Pangbourne
Third full week in July, Monday to Thursday

It could truly be said that the Swan Voyage at the end of July, as it leaves Sunbury for Pangbourne, is a majestic sight. The first two of the rowing boats belong to the Queen, and in the first of these is the Queen's Swanherd, the boat sporting a banner with both the royal initials and a swan, the men all in their red jerseys. These first two boats are followed by the two belonging to the Vintners' Company, commanded by their Swan Marker in green livery and, following these, the two boats belonging to the Dyers' Company with their blue livery and flag. Together they have the task of upping all the swans on the River Thames between Sunbury and Pangbourne. The time of year has been chosen to allow the recently hatched cygnets to reach a manageable size. All the swans encountered are 'upped' (turned on their backs) and their beaks checked to see who they belong to. Those belonging to the Queen are those without marks; those with two nicks belong to the Vinters', and those with one nick to the Dyers'. The cygnets are then marked appropriately, or not if they are royal birds, and their wings are clipped. Cygnets of mixed parentage are divided equally between cob and pen and marked accordingly, but if there is an odd one it is given the cob's marking. The voyage travels slowly up the river to Pangbourne, stopping overnight on the way, and not forgetting to make a salute to the Queen at Windsor Castle when it comes into view, with the words: 'Her Majesty the Queen, Seigneur of Swans'.

Swans have been regarded as royal property since the 14th century and have been carefully protected as such. The unlicensed killing of a swan is a crime, even if found in the open water. There are exceptions to the royal prerogative, and both the Vintners' and the Dyers' were allowed swan-rights on the River Thames.

Both companies were keen to protect their own rights, and they organised the annual Swan Voyage up the Thames to make sure that any additions to their own 'game' of swans were duly marked as such. In the 17th and 18th centuries, it was a matter of some great feasting and ceremonial, when both companies had their own magnificent barges.

It is the responsibility of the Royal Swanherd and the two company wardens to look after the swans throughout the year and, as one of the purposes of caring for the swans was to serve them up at banquets, so the practice is still continued by both companies at their elaborate and splendid dinners. The Vintners' is called the Five Kings' Feast, commemorating an occasion in 1363 when it is said that five monarchs sat down as guests of Henry Picard, Vintner and Lord Mayor. These were Edward III of England; David, King of Scotland; John, King of France; Waldemar, King of Denmark; and Amadeus, King of Cyprus. The Vintners' toast is always followed by 'five cheers'.

Those who have wondered at the pub name *The Swan with Two Necks* need wonder no more. It is a corruption of the 'Swan with Two Nicks': one that belonged to the Vintners' Company.

Tar Barrels Parade

Allendale Town, Northumberland

31 December

On New Year's Eve in Allendale Town, they see the old year out and the new year in with a most spectacular custom. The men, all dressed in fanciful attire and known as 'guisers', throng the busy pubs throughout the evening, adding to the conviviality. Shortly before midnight, the pubs turn out into the streets to see the fun. The band strikes up and the guisers, who have now become tar-barrellers, arrive bearing their 'kits' – barrels sawn in three and full of flammable materials. These are ignited and the band leads the tar-barrellers briskly round the town to return to the square, where the ceremonial bonfire has been prepared. At the stroke of midnight, the guisers throw the flaming contents of the barrels onto the fire, and the assembled inhabitants and visitors join in the singing of *Auld Lang Syne*. Thereafter, the guisers busy themselves first-footing around the town.

Tichborne Dole

Tichborne, Hampshire

25 March

Every year on Lady Day, one of the country's oldest charities is dispensed from the steps of Tichborne House in Hampshire by the heirs of the Tichborne Estate. Every inhabitant of Tichborne or Cheriton who presents him- or herself at the House is entitled to receive a gallon of flour. This is dispensed after it has been blessed by a priest and a short service has been held.

That the charity is continued today after nearly 800 years is understandable when you look into its strange history. At some time in the 12th century, Lady Mabella de Tichborne, a woman renowned for her goodness and charity, lay dying. She asked her husband if he would set aside some land after her death; from the wheat grown on this, bread would be made and given out each Lady Day to the people of the parish of Tichborne and Cheriton. Sir Roger de Tichborne took a burning brand from the fire and presented it to his wife. He told her that she could have as much land for the purpose of her dole as she could walk round before the flame went out. Helped outside by her maids but unable to walk, Lady Mabella managed to crawl round twenty-three acres of land before the brand burnt out. The land she encircled became known afterwards as 'the crawls', and though she was to die shortly after courageously marking out the land, she was strong enough to leave her husband a warning. These are the words she is reputed to have said:

> 'Let no man dare to break this solemn promise, or tamper with so sacred a gift, for then a curse shall fall upon him and upon his house. The fortunes of the family shall fail, the name of Tichborne shall be changed and the family shall die out. As a sign hereof there shall be born a generation of seven sons, followed by one of seven daughters.'

All went well for 600 years or so, while the dole was faithfully given out on Lady Day, but in the 1790s such a flock of supplicants came to Tichborne Park that the heir, Sir Henry, decided to divert the proceeds of the crawl lands to the church. He duly had seven sons, five of them dying young, and then part of the house collapsed. The eldest son and heir changed his name to Tichborne-Doughty and fathered seven daughters, but wisely restored the dole in 1835, though the curse had not fully worked itself out yet. The nephew and heir to the title, Sir Roger Tichborne, disappeared or was drowned at sea in 1859. When his father died in 1862, his mother refused to believe in Sir Roger's death and advertised in the papers for any news of her son's whereabouts. The man who stepped forward and claimed to be the missing nephew became known as the Tichborne Claimant, about whom books have been written. Though the mother said she recognised him, and he was able to answer questions about the family with remarkable facility, he lost the action for his claim to the title and the estate in 1872, and in 1874 he was imprisoned for fourteen years for fraud and misrepresentation. He was Thomas Castro, a Wapping butcher known as 'Bullocky Orton', and he cost the Tichborne family tens of thousands of pounds in legal expenses.

The dole has not been allowed to lapse since, though it was threatened in the late 1940s when bread and flour was rationed, and the family couldn't stump up the necessary coupons. The matter reached the press and thousands of coupons were donated by concerned readers, before the Ministry of Food made a special dispensation to their rules to allow the dole to be distributed. Lady Mabella's heroic crawl will not be forgotten.

Tolling the Devil's Knell

Dewsbury, Yorkshire

24 December

A couple of hours before midnight at All Saints' Church in Dewsbury, the bell-ringers take it in turns to toll the Devil's Knell. The tenor bell rings out once for every year since the birth of Christ, down to the present year, and the last toll is timed to fall on the stroke of midnight. Careful preparation is required beforehand to keep count of the bells tolled, which are marked off on a score-sheet, while a watch is kept on the time to ensure the last toll and midnight come together.

The custom is said to date back variously to the 13th century, or to the 16th, as the expiation for a murder committed by either a member of the Saville family, or Thomas de Soothill; he died in 1535 and gave the bell, which became known afterwards as Black Tom of Soothill, as a penance. Whenever the custom began originally, it was revived in 1828 after a lapse of a few years, and has continued almost without interruption ever since. The idea is that when Jesus was born Satan died, and that unless his death is tolled every year, with the addition of a chime for the current year, Satan is likely to come back. A tally is kept of the annual tolling, duly signed by the bell-ringers, and afterwards the parish is said to be free from any devilish pranks for the next twelve months.

Tom Bawcock's Eve

Mousehole, Cornwall

23 December

A truly local event is celebrated at the Ship, in Mousehole, on the day before Christmas Eve. This is Tom Bawcock's Eve, when a cook from the pub, or a local restaurant, makes a couple of huge 'starry-gazy' pies, from seven different sorts of fish. Portions of these pies, with fishes' heads and tails sticking out of them, are handed round to the customers while the song commemorating the event is sung. This goes as follows:

> *A merry place you may believe*
> *Was Mousehole on Tom Bawcock's Eve*
> *To be there then, who wadna' wish*
> *And sup on seven sorts of fish*
> > *(CHORUS)*
>
> *With margy broth us cleared the path*
> *And lances for a fry*
> *And then us 'ad a bit of scad*
> *And starry-gazy pie*
>
> *Next came fermaads braw thirsty jaads*
> *As made our oozles dry*
> *And ling and hake enough to make*
> *A running shark to sigh*
>
> *As hake we'd clunk as health were drunk*
> *With bumpers breemin' high*
> *And when up came Tom Bawcock's name*
> *Us praised en to the sky*

It is said that some two hundred years ago, the fishermen of Mousehole had been unable to find any fish, and the people in the little fishing port were facing starvation. One of their number, Tom Bawcock, suddenly arrived with a large catch consisting of seven different sorts of fish, and became the saviour of Mousehole.

Turning the Devil's Stone

Shebbear, near Holsworthy, Devon

5 November

While everywhere else in the country on 5 November people are commemorating the memory of Guy Fawkes and his perfidious gunpowder plot, the villagers of Shebbear in Devon are preparing to turn the Devil's Stone. The bell-ringers go to the church at about 8 o'clock in the evening, where they ring out a violently discordant peal of bells. That done, they make their way out of the church and, with the aid of crowbars, apply themselves to the task of turning the Shebbear, or Devil's, Stone nearby. After this considerable exertion, they can rest from their labours, secure in the knowledge that Shebbear is safe from harm in the coming year.

While it is not known for how long the practice of turning the stone has been going on, there is a wealth of legend surrounding it and as to how it arrived. The stone itself is about six feet long and is said to weigh a ton. It is not from a local rock formation and is, in fact, an erratic – that is, a stone from elsewhere, such as those deposited in the Ice Age. One theory is that it may have been an altar stone brought by a pagan cult, in the way that the Druids brought stones from Wales to Stonehenge in Wiltshire, though there is no evidence for this. Another is that it was dropped by the Devil himself when he was cast out of heaven by St Michael, hence the clamour of discordant bells to frighten him away. Finally, there is the theory that it was quarried as the foundation stone for Henscott Church nearby and was moved to Shebbear by the Devil or some supernatural force, and that every time it was retrieved, it mysteriously turned up at Shebbear again, so was finally left there.

It is said that the turning was neglected once in the First World War, when misfortune immediately descended on the village. Again, in 1940, when most of the able-bodied men were away, they failed to turn the stone and the war news suddenly became so threatening that they hastened to make good their neglect. It is unlikely that it won't be turned again in the future.

Tyburn Walk
From St Sepulchre's Church, London EC4 to Hyde Park Corner
Last Sunday in April

At 3 o'clock in the afternoon on the last Sunday in April, a group of Catholic worshippers assemble outside St Sepulchre's church, opposite the site of Newgate Prison (now the Old Bailey), in preparation for a procession to Hyde Park Corner, the site of the Tyburn Gallows. They walk the route that the condemned took from the prison to their execution, stopping at a number of churches on the way, including St Ethelreda's in Ely Place and St Patrick's in Soho Square.

Of the many thousands of those hanged at Tyburn, a number were Catholic martyrs; the walk is in memory of the 105 Catholics who were put to death here and at other sites in London, such as Tower Hill and St Paul's churchyard, during the Reformation. It is a pilgrimage of about 2½ miles and concludes with a sermon outside the Tyburn Convent in Bayswater Road, adjacent to the site of the gallows at a spot marked by three brass triangles let into the pavement on the corner of Edgeware Road. The last execution to be carried out at Tyburn was in 1783, and thereafter the executions were carried out at Newgate Prison until it was demolished.

Tynwald Ceremony

St Johns, Isle of Man

*5 July (or nearest Monday,
if 5 July is a Saturday or Sunday)*

Although the Tynwald Ceremony is a state occasion, it is one that has a direct link with Norse assemblies ten centuries earlier. On or about what is Old Midsummer's Day, there is a short service in St John's Chapel; the Lieutenant-Governor, preceded by his Swordbearer, then leads the civic and religious dignitaries to Tynwald Hill, their pathway strewn with rushes. He takes his place on the seat of the Norse Kings beside the Bishop of Sodor and Man. He is surrounded by the two Deemsters, or judges; the representatives of the Manx Parliament, the House of Keys (from Manx *kiare-as-feed*, meaning four and twenty); and the vicars of the island's parishes. Before the ceremony begins, the assembly is 'fenced' by the Chief Coroner: that is, he orders that those present should not 'quarrel, brawl, or make disturbance' while the Tynwald is in session, 'on pain of death'. Then a summary of the laws passed in the last year is read out, in Manx and English. After this, the whole gathering has to give its verbal approval, which it does with three rousing cheers for the Queen.

The Tynwald, roughly meaning place of assembly, takes place on Tynwald Hill, constructed on the summit of an ancient burial mound and thought to have been a gathering place even before the Vikings came. The earliest recorded ceremony here was in 1417, but the Vikings ruled the island from about AD 900 onwards, and it was their meeting place when Manx laws were orally declaimed rather than written down in books.

Wassailing the Apple Trees

Carhampton, Somerset

17 January

Somerset is cider country, and there is good reason for the people of Carhampton to keep alive the custom of wassailing the apple trees, as they do on old Twelfth Night. There are only a few apple trees left in an orchard now sacrificed for houses, but the regulars of the local pub, the Butcher's Arms, make sure the tradition is honoured. After mulling some cider, they take it out to a selected tree, where they drink its health and sing the wassail song:

> *Old apple tree, we wassail thee,*
> *And hoping thou wilt bear*
> *For the Lord doth know where we shall be*
> *Till apples come another year.*
>
> *For to bloom well, and to bear well*
> *So let us merry be.*
> *Let every man take off his hat*
> *And shout to the old apple tree!*
>
> *Old apple tree, we wassail thee,*
> *And hoping thou wilt bear*
> *Hatfuls, capfuls, three-bushel bagfuls*
> *And a little heap under the stairs!*

Then to cries of 'Hip, hip hooray!', some of the cider is poured over the roots of the tree, and some pieces of toast, soaked in cider, are placed on forks in the branches. Finally, shotguns are fired through the tree to frighten away evil spirits. After that, the regulars return to the pub, having assured an abundant apple crop for the coming year.

To wassail is to wish good health (Old English *was hal* or *hael*), and the custom of wassailing, the drinking of each other's good health from a wooden bowl, was a common custom on New Year's Eve and Twelfth Night. Among country people, it was extended to farm animals, crops, bees and even apple trees, particularly in the West Country.

Wayfarers' Dole
St Cross Hospital,
Winchester, Hampshire
Every weekday

The wayfarer's dole, given out daily at the Hospital of St Cross on the outskirts of Winchester, has been dispensed here for 800 years and is one of the oldest of such charities still continued. On any weekday, the first thirty-two supplicants who apply at the porter's lodge receive a portion of bread and a measure of beer, dispensed from an ancient horn cup bearing a silver cross.

The hospital of St Cross was founded by Bishop Henry de Blois in 1136, for the support of thirteen poor men, who were to be provided 'with garments and beds suitable for their infirmities, good wheaten bread daily of the weight of five marks, and three dishes at dinner, and one at supper suitable to the day, and drink of good stuff'.

In 1446 Cardinal Henry Beaufort added an almshouse for a smaller 'Order of Average Poverty'. The Blois Brethren wear black gowns with the silver cross of the Knights Hospitallers of St John, and the Beaufort Brethren wear dark-red gowns and the cardinal's badge. The hospital's charity was freely offered to outsiders, and in Henry de Blois' day, a hundred persons were fed every day, though the number reached twice that at a later date. Today, the dole itself and the numbers who receive it, are restricted to the small portions offered at the gate to the first thirty-two needy supplicants.

Weighing the Mayor
The Guildhall, High Wycombe, Buckinghamshire
Late in May

One of the first duties performed by the Mayor of High Wycombe is to be weighed in public. This takes place following the election and immediately after formally taking office. On the date in question, a procession of civic dignitaries emerges from the Guildhall, outside which a large tripod has been erected; from this is suspended a chair hanging from a scale, much as is used in fish markets. The new incumbent in office sits in the chair, the weight is checked by the Inspector of Weights and Measures, and read out in a loud voice by the Beadle. Following the mayor, 'any other official who desires to be weighed' takes their place in the chair and is duly weighed, including the retiring mayor. The previous year's weight is read out, and if he or she has gained or lost weight, this is made plain by the addition of the words 'and *some* more' or 'and *no* more', accordingly. The assembled onlookers greet the news with cheers or boos, depending upon the loss or gain, on the assumption that those who've gained weight in office haven't been looking after the interests of others, but only their own.

Though it is recorded that Queen Elizabeth I made some pointed remarks about the corpulence of the civic dignitaries of High Wycombe, there is no evidence that the weighing of the mayor dated from her reign. There are records from Queen Victoria's reign, however, and certainly it is an annual civic event much enjoyed by the public, and one which is a reminder to the mayor to watch his weight while in office.

Well-Dressing

Tissington, Derbyshire

Ascension Day

The custom of well-dressing is popular all over Derbyshire, but the well-dressing in the village of Tissington is probably the most famous, and certainly the most visually striking. There are five wells in Tissington, and each one is lovingly and painstakingly dressed for Ascension Day in preparations that last a full week beforehand. On Ascension Day itself, there is a morning service in the church, followed by a procession round all the wells in turn, each one being individually blessed, often by different clergymen.

Wells were sacred places long before the birth of Christianity, and it is not known when the wells at Tissington were first dressed with flowers, though it is likely they were revered as sacred from time immemorial. Some say the present custom began following the plague in 1350, which mysteriously spared the village of Tissington, and which the villagers attributed to the purity of the water. Others say that it began in 1615, when there was a terrible drought which the people were able to survive because the wells never dried up. Certainly, the custom was thought worthy of note by a visitor in the 1750s and again in 1818. In the 1860s it was carried out much as it is today. Large-scale coloured drawings, either of previously-used designs or original ones, of biblical pictures, symbols and scriptural texts are painstakingly recreated on large clay-covered boards. This is done, as in mosaics, by pressing in flowers, beans and chips of coloured local stone. The night before Ascension Day, the boards are erected around their respective wells to construct a highly colourful shrine. Since no artificial flowers are used and the clay is susceptible to the weather, the well-dressing shrines last no more than a few days and are obviously at their best on the morning of Ascension Day.

Other notable well-dressings take place in Buxton and Wirksworth in Derbyshire, but the custom is also known in Gloucestershire and Staffordshire.

Welsh National Eisteddfod
Wales, variable locations

August

The Welsh National Eisteddfod takes place in August, in a different location every year. It is a celebration of Welsh language and culture, and a number of bardic chairs are awarded, principally for poetry. It is presided over by the Arch Druid of the Gorsedd, and opened when he unsheathes his ceremonial sword and demands in Welsh: *'A oes Heddwych?'* – Is there peace? With the massed response of *'Heddwych!'* – Peace! – from the assembly, the proceedings get under way.

The National Eisteddfod (meaning, roughly, a sitting) in its present form goes back to 1880, though the history of eisteddfodau goes back to a time before the Christian era. The first recorded eisteddfod was held in Cardigan in 1176, presided over by the Lord Rhys. Another was held in 1568, and the first to be held along present-day lines took place in Corwen in 1789. The proceedings are conducted entirely in the Welsh language and recent innovations have seen a chair awarded for a novel.

Widow's Bun Ceremony
Widow's Son, 75 Devons Road, London E3
Good Friday

The Widow's Son is one of the few London pubs to take its name from a living legend, and once a year on Good Friday a custom is honoured that perpetuates the legend. A sailor is invited to add a hot-cross bun to a collection that hangs from the ceiling, in memory of a sailor-son who never returned as promised for Easter. When this simple but moving service has been performed, hot-cross buns are handed out to all the customers.

The story has it that a widow lived in a cottage on the site of the pub, and that her son went off to sea, his return being expected next Easter.

When Easter came round, the widow baked some hot-cross buns for him, and when he didn't show up, she kept one. Though the boy never returned, she did the same every year until she died, by which time the house had become known as the Bun Shop. The pub which took the name of the Widow's Son was built in the late 19th century and the collection of buns hanging from the ceiling is a bizarre sight. It is perhaps best summed up by Harold Adshead, a gentleman whose verses grace many a London pub and whose concluding stanza on the subject goes:

> *The buns hung high for all to see,*
> *A blackened mess above;*
> *A truly strange epitome*
> *Of patient mother love.*

Wroth Silver
Knightlow Hill, Ryton-on-Dunsmore, Warwickshire
11 November

This is an ancient custom that takes place before dawn on the feast of St Martin, at Knightlow Hill, between Coventry and Dunchurch. The representatives of the twenty-five parishes of the Hundred of Knightlow are summoned by the agent of the lord of the manor, the Duke of Buccleuch, to pay the wroth silver due before the rising of the sun. As each parish is named, and the amount read out, the representative steps forward and throws the money in a hollow stone, repeating the words 'Wroth Silver'. Having discharged their duties, the parish representatives then all repair to a local hostelry for breakfast. Speeches are made, toasts drunk in rum and hot milk, and churchwarden pipes are handed out.

Wroth silver is money paid to the lord in lieu of castle-ward, that is, a feudal obligation in return for protection, castle-ward (or guard) being knight-service for defending the lord's castle. It is said to be one of the oldest continuously performed customs in Britain and was already an established practice in 1236, though thought to have begun much earlier. Certainly, a Hundred is one of the most ancient legal subdivisions of a shire. Defaulters are warned that non-payment means 'forfeiture of 100 pence for every penny, or a White Bull with red ears and red nose'. The reference to the bull seems to take the ceremony back to a time when the old white cattle of England were common, though some think it suggests that the wroth silver was paid to give the local people the right to drive their cattle over his lordship's land. It is said that a defaulter was made to produce a bull in the nineteenth century, though being the wrong colour this was found unacceptable, and likewise the story is apocryphal.

Whatever the origins, the custom is still honoured, the wroth silver still paid, and breakfast is still enjoyed.

Other customs mentioned briefly

Burrator Reservoir Ceremony, Burrator Reservoir, near Yelverton, Devon; a day in July. A commemoration of Sir Francis Drake's provision of a water supply from the River Meavy to Plymouth in 1591.

Corby Pole Fair, Corby, Northamptonshire; Whit Monday every 20 years (next one in 2002). Miscreants carried on a pole (ladies in a chair) to town stocks.

Cyclists' Memorial Service, Cyclists' War Memorial, Meriden, Warwickshire; Sunday morning nearest 21 May. Cyclists come from all over the country to remember their dead in two world wars at their own memorial, erected in 1921 at their own expense.

Denby Dale Pie, Denby Dale, Yorkshire. Huge pie baked occasionally on uncertain dates to celebrate unusual event, first in 1788.

Glove is Up, Honiton, Devon; Tuesday after St Margaret's Eve (19 July). Town crier announces opening of the fair while holding gilded leather glove atop a 12-foot, garlanded pole.

Horse Shoe Tax, Oakham Castle, Oakham, Rutland. Collection of horseshoes demanded as taxes from every peer visiting Oakham for the first time.

Jankyn Smith's Charity, St Mary's, Bury St Edmunds, Suffolk; Tuesday nearest 28 June. Requiem service said for wealthy benefactor of the town, followed by a modest reception for almshouse residents in the Guildhall.

John Stow's Quill Pen, St Andrew Undershaft, Leadenhall Street, London EC3; on or near 5 April. Replacing a quill pen by civic dignitary in hand of Stow's effigy inside church.

Little Edith's Treat, Piddinghoe, near Lewes, East Sussex; 19 July. Anniversary treat for children in memory of Little Edith Croft, who died aged 13 months in 1868.

Maids' Money, St Mary's Church, Reading, Berkshire; around Easter. Charity divided among 'faithful maidservants'.

Mari Lwyd, Llangynwyd, Glamorgan, and elsewhere in South Wales; Christmas Eve to Twelfth Night. Hooded horse, or gray mare in Welsh, who knocks up householders over Christmas to bring luck for New Year.

Marvyn Dole, Ufton Court, Ufton Nervet, near Reading, Berkshire; Maundy Thursday. Dame Elisabeth Marvyn's Charity of bread and cloth handed out to named parishioners by vicar.

Old Man's Day, Braughing, near Bishop's Stortford, Hertfordshire; 2 October. Commemoration of Matthew Wall brought back to life on way to be buried in 16th century, when rector and local children follow coffin.

Pipe Walk, from St Mary Redcliffe to Knowle, Bristol; a Saturday afternoon in September. Commemorative walk in thanksgiving for spring water piped from Knowle to St Mary's parish following path of pipe.

Straw Bear Day, Whittlesey, Cambridgeshire; Saturday nearest Plough Monday. Man dressed as straw bear collects money for charity in streets.

Swearing on the Horns, Old Wrestlers Tavern, North Road, Highgate, London N6; Wednesday before Spring Bank Holiday and Wednesday nine days after Summer Bank Holiday. Elaborate oath demanded from customers who receive a certificate and part with money for charity.

The Straw Bear doing the rounds at Whittlesey

Calendar

Please note that the moveable feasts are separate from the months, as Shrovetide can fall in February or March, Easter in March or April and Ascension in April or May.

JANUARY

6th	Baddeley Cake, Drury Lane Theatre, London WC2
6th	Haxey Hood Game, Haxey, Lincolnshire
17th	Wassailing the Apple Trees, Carhampton, Somerset

FEBRUARY

2nd	Forty Shilling Day, Wotton, near Dorking, Surrey
3rd	Blessing the Throats, St Ethelreda, Ely Place, London EC1
First Monday after Candlemas (2nd)	Hurling the Silver Ball, St Ives, Cornwall

Shrovetide

Shrove Tuesday and Ash Wednesday	Ashbourne Ball Game, Ashbourne, Derbyshire
Shrove Tuesday and second Saturday following	Hurling, St Columb Major, Cornwall
Shrove Tuesday	Olney Pancake Race, Olney, Buckinghamshire
Shrove Tuesday	Purbeck Marblers and Stonecutters Day, Corfe Castle, Dorset

MARCH

25th	Tichborne Dole, Tichborne, Hampshire
Third Thursday	Kiplingcotes Derby, South Dalton, Yorkshire

Weekday near 31st	Oranges and Lemons Service, St Clement Danes, London WC2

Easter

Maundy Thursday	Royal Maundy, different cathedral annually
Good Friday	Marbles Championship, Tinsley Green, near Crawley, Sussex
Good Friday	Widow's Bun Ceremony, Widow's Son, 75 Devons Road, London E3
Easter Saturday	Britannia Coconut Dancers, Bacup, Lancashire
Easter Monday	Biddenden Dole or Maids' Charity, Biddenden, Kent
Easter Monday	Hare Pie Scramble and Bottle-Kicking, Hallaton, Leicestershire
Second Tuesday after Easter	Hocktide, Hungerford, Berkshire

APRIL

30th – 3rd May	Minehead Hobby Horse, Minehead, Somerset
Last Sunday	Tyburn Walk, from St Sepulchre's Church, London EC4 to Hyde Park Corner

MAY

1st (and 19th September)	Garland Dressing, Charlton-on-Otmoor, Oxfordshire
1st	May Morning, Magdalen College, Oxford
1st	Padstow Hobby Horse, Padstow, Cornwall
8th	Helston Furry Dance, Helston, Cornwall
13th	Abbotsbury Garland Day, Abbotsbury, Dorset
18th or Wednesday nearest	Dunting the Freeholder, Newbiggin-by-the-Sea, Northumberland
29th	Arbor Day, Aston-on-Clun, Shropshire
29th	Grovely Rights Day, Great Wishford, Wiltshire

29th	Garland Day, Castleton, Derbyshire
Saturday nearest 29th	Battle of Neville's Cross, Durham Cathedral
Spring Bank Holiday Monday	Cheese Rolling, Cooper's Hill Brockworth, Gloucestershire
Spring Bank Holiday Monday (every 3 years)	Common Walk, Laugharne, Dyfed
Spring Bank Holiday Monday	Greenhill Bower and Court of Array, Lichfield, Staffordshire
Spring Bank Holiday weekend	Hunting the Earl of Rone, Combe Martin, Devon
Spring Bank Holiday Tuesday (every 3 years)	Maypole Raising, Barwick-in-Elmet, Yorkshire
Late in month	Weighing the Mayor, The Guildhall, High Wycombe, Buckinghamshire

Ascensiontide

Ascension Eve	Penny Hedge, Whitby, Yorkshire
Ascension Day	Well-Dressing, Tissington, Derbyshire
Whit Sunday evening	Bread and Cheese Throwing, St Briavels, Gloucestershire
Whit Monday	Dicing for Bibles, St Ives, Cambridgeshire
Whit Monday (every leap year)	Dunmow Flitch Trials, Great Dunmow, Essex

JUNE

Friday following Spring Bank Holiday	Cotswold Olympic Games, Chipping Campden, Gloucestershire
Saturday nearest 19th	Mayor of Ock Street, Abingdon, Oxfordshire
Week of 2nd Wednesday	Appleby Horse Fair, Appleby, Cumbria
21st	Midsummer Day Ritual, Stonehenge, Wiltshire
Third Saturday	Bawming the Thorn, Appleton, near Warrington, Cheshire
Week following 29th	Lot-meadow Drawing, Yarnton, Oxfordshire

JULY

5th or nearest Monday if 5th a Saturday or Sunday	Tynwald Ceremony, St Johns, Isle of Man
First or second Saturday	Admiralty Court, Rochester, Kent
Second Wednesday	Pretty Maid's Charity, Holsworthy, Devon
Second Saturday	Durham Miner's Gala, Durham
Third full week	Swan Upping, River Thames from Sunbury to Pangbourne
25th	Ebernoe Horn Fair, near Petworth, Sussex
25th (every five years)	John Knill's Charity, St Ives, Cornwall

AUGUST

1st or nearest date depending on tides	Doggett's Coat and Badge Race, between London and Chelsea Bridges
First Wednesday and following days	Knights of the Old Green Competition, Southampton, Hampshire
First week	Grand Wardmote of the Woodmen of Arden, Meriden, Warwickshire
Saturday before first Monday	St Wilfrid's Feast Procession, Ripon, Yorkshire
24th	St Bartholomew's Bun Race, St Bartholomew's Hospital, Sandwich, Kent
Saturday nearest 24th	Burning Bartle, West Witton, Yorkshire
Last Sunday	Eyam Plague Memorial, Eyam, Derbyshire
A date in month	Welsh National Eisteddford, variable locations

SEPTEMBER

1st	Colchester Oyster Ceremony, Colchester, Essex
A Saturday near 8th	Sheriff's Ride, Lichfield, Staffordshire

First Monday following the Sunday after 4th	Abbots Bromley Horn Dance, Abbots Bromley, Staffordshire
Saturday nearest 18th	Egremont Crab Fair, Egremont, Cumbria
19th	Clipping the Church, St Mary's, Painswick, Gloucestershire
19th (and 1st May)	Garland Dressing, Charlton-on-Otmoor, Oxfordshire
27th and onwards to Shrove Tuesday	Hornblowing, Bainbridge, Yorkshire

OCTOBER

31st	Antrobus Souling Play, Antrobus, Cheshire

NOVEMBER

5th	Bonfire Night, Ottery St Mary, Devon
5th	Lewes Bonfire Night, Lewes, Sussex
5th	Turning the Devil's Stone, Shebbear, near Holsworthy, Devon
Thursday nearest 5th	Guy Fawkes Carnival, Bridgwater, Somerset
11th	Firing the Poppers, Fenny Stratford, Buckinghamshire
11th	Wroth Silver, Knightlow Hill, Ryton-on-Dunsmore, Warwickshire

DECEMBER

Second Sunday	Broughton Tin Can Band, Broughton, Northamptonshire
23rd	Tom Bawcock's Eve, Mousehole, Cornwall
24th	Tolling the Devil's Knell, Dewsbury, Yorkshire
Boxing Day	Marshfield Paper Boys, Marshfield, Gloucestershire
31st	Tar Barrels Parade, Allendale Town, Northumberland

DAILY

Throughout year, 9 pm	Hornblowing, Ripon, Yorkshire
Weekdays	Wayfarers' Dole, St Cross Hospital, Winchester, Hampshire

N.B. Many of the above events move to a Saturday or Monday if they fall on a Sunday.

Index